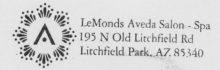

LeMonds Aveda Salon - Spa
195 N Old Litchfield Rd
Litchfield Park, AZ 85340

**FULL OF BREATHTAKING BEAUTY**
and engaging stories, this collection celebrates the places, traditions, and mythol-
ogies surrounding the healing benefits of
heat. Featuring more than 50 locations—
from an ancient holy hot spring bubbling
out of terraced pools in Turkey, to a cozy
sauna perched high on a snowcapped
ridge in Alaska, to a wooden hot tub built
on a schooner that sails through Iceland's
arctic waters—these pages overflow
with idyllic landscapes and rejuvenating
inspiration.

Sprinkled throughout are simple practices
for incorporating the restorative powers
of heat, steam, and water into daily life,
including rejuvenating bath recipes, healing steam rituals, and herbal remedies
that encourage well-being at home.

Perfect for outdoor enthusiasts, travelers,
and anyone with a spirit of adventure,
these pages invite you to immerse yourself in the restorative and invigorating
power of nature.

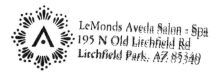

**HEALING WITH HEAT**
*Saunas, Hot Springs & Baths*

# RMAL

LINDSEY BRO

CHRONICLE BOOKS
SAN FRANCISCO

Library of Congress Cataloging-in-Publication Data available.

ISBN 978-1-7972-1857-1

Manufactured in China.

Design by Vanessa Dina.
Typeset by Frank Brayton.

10 9 8 7 6 5 4 3 2 1

Chronicle books and gifts are available at special quantity discounts
to corporations, professional associations, literacy programs, and other
organizations. For details and discount information, please contact our
premiums department at corporatesales@chroniclebooks.com or at
1-800-759-0190.

Chronicle Books LLC
680 Second Street
San Francisco, California 94107
www.chroniclebooks.com

For
those
who
seek
warmth.

# CONTENTS

Heat as healing is ancient. Since time immemorial we have sought warmth as a way to return home. From the hot, enveloping atmosphere of the sauna; to the deep, embracing allure of geothermal waters; to the sometimes contradictory, yet always beloved and enduring initiation of bathhouses around the world, we as humans appear to crave the sacred rites of water, in all its forms, as a way to remember.

The history of sauna and bathing is, really, a history of humanity. What began as warm stones heated in the fire and brought inside (or placed under hides and tarps) has become, in a way, a massive industry. In another way, its essence remains the same—a way to warm ourselves when it's cold outside, to find respite, to connect; to keep traditions alive, to honor our ancestors, to sit in awe of nature; to cleanse, to detoxify, to heal.

While bathing began long before the Greeks and Romans, they were the ones to put in the hard hours that elevated it from chore to egalitarian art form. Both physical and metaphysical, the benefits of bathing are as restorative as they are reviving—a reminder that wellness is an ever-evolving, holistic, and individual journey. Though chronologically a far cry from the times of Sparta, where spa culture began, today's modern bathhouses are very much still centered around the communal as well as the personal experience of bathing.

Today, there is a renewal and revival of soak and sweat culture on the rise. Though it may be better thought of as a remembering because, around the world, the pastime of thermic bathing has never really faded, and as individuals discover and embrace it for themselves, their approach often depends on their perspective. Is it a health hack for optimal wellness? An age-old method and modality of self-care? Recreation? Or, perhaps, it's something more.

With the power to link us to our collective and individual cultural heritage, sauna is deceivingly transformative. For such a simple act—sitting in a hot room for a period of time—its iterations are nearly endless. Not surprisingly, *sauna*, a proto-Baltic-Finnic word originating from *savńa* or *sakna* and linked to the Estonian *saun*, has never really been about the structure. For some, it's closer to a religion than an activity tacked on to the end of a session at the gym. For others, it's an integrated practice. For many, it's a way to slow down, to find presence, and to tap into the healing power of heat.

In some circles, they say sauna is meant to make you hate your life so that, when you finally emerge, you really love your life. More than anything, though, the greatest gift of sauna may be that it fosters a deep sense of connection. Galvanizing for body, mind, and spirit, connection gives us a sense of purpose; it reminds us we are not alone; it provides community, a sense of belonging, and a deep knowing that we are part of something greater.

This modern world is busy, polluted, and oftentimes hectic, if not bordering on chaotic. Simple and still, sauna is a sweet antidote. A revolution in a way, and a salve for our ever-growing solastalgia in the face of change. Tactile and immediate, sweating is a physical and emotional release: it cleanses the body, removes toxins, stimulates the lymphatic system, and stresses our bodies in beneficial ways, making them stronger and more resilient. As a form of meditation, sauna offers us the chance to remove the stimuli, to disconnect from the devices, and to process our own internal worlds. By pushing ourselves to the edges of our discomfort, we expand our ability to feel—and our ability to feel is in direct relation to our ability to experience life.

Like all art projects, outdoor saunas are not bound by rules. There is no right or wrong way to build one and no shape that has to be adhered to; in a sense, building a sauna captures the ultimate DIY ethos of using what you have and finding a way to make it work. An apt metaphor for life, each sauna is incredibly unique and can take on nearly any form. Expensive infrared heaters, a wood-fired converted horse trailer, a small shed with an electric stove—they are all saunas. As the Finns would say, it's *löyly* (from the Finnish word meaning "a cloud of steam") that is really considered the spirit and life force of a sauna anyway. As with anything, an outdoor sauna will be in conversation with nature and there is a responsibility to be conscious of the materials chosen and the impact of its design on the natural world.

In many ways, water holds memory and, like ritual, water connects us to a shared history—to times, people, and places we will never experience. Reverence and intention bring magic to the mundane,

imbuing the acts of sauna and bathing with a sense of intercon-
nection, reminding us we are all equal and all the same. After all,
human beings are not machines. We are part of nature, not apart from
it. And we have always been drawn to, dependent on, and fascinated
by the natural world. Biophilia, or this love of life, is an innate, biolog-
ically driven need to commune with the natural world, experiencing its
regenerative, restorative, and spiritual powers.

Steeped in lore, the phenomenon of naturally occurring warm
waters found in seemingly inexplicable places used to be a thing of
mythology and fabled origin stories. Today, we have a more scientific
understanding of hot springs and thermal waters—they exist because
of shifting tectonic plates, heated groundwater, and the collection
of minerals. However, folklore is powerful. Stories of healing waters
have been passed down through generations, and it's these stories
that feel most true. After all, magic, mythology, and science are
surprisingly close, and surreal healing waters continue to be found all
over the world, making the promise of the fabled Fountain of Youth
seem more probable than ever.

Today, warm waters are still the stuff of legend, enticing us with the
promise of elusive coordinates, a bit of adventure, and the reward of
a relaxing, restorative soak. More often than not, hot springs seem
to fall into one of three categories: wild, natural springs; built-up,
human-made springs; or somewhere in between. No one is better
than the others—it's a matter of context and preference—but it's
undeniable that the added amenity of the natural world has its own
allure.

Hot springs, in some form or another, exist on every continent and
have been important parts of Indigenous and Native cultures for
centuries. From ceremonial purification to healing the sick, warm
waters have been part of life, considered sacred, and protected as
such. As questions of land rights and water sovereignty continue to
be addressed, respecting Indigenous knowledge and practices of
nature and land is more pressing than ever.

To be sure, immersing ourselves in the natural world is a good thing—
and perhaps the details about why are not the important part. People
used to soak in waters without knowing why they felt better after, but
still knew that they did. They did not have to cross-reference the data,
but rather moved from an intuitive, trusting space: One that believed

nature ultimately holds the key to our healing. Later, modern science entered the picture, and we now know the more we interact with nature, the higher our levels of satisfaction, gratitude, productivity, vitality, and balance become.

In truth, the salve of thermic bathing—which includes sauna, hot springs, and bathhouse culture—is that it is one of the many practices of letting go. It's all divine, and, with no attachment to the past or the future, sweating is a return to the pre-formal, a space full of nothing but possibility and potential.

It's no wonder we still crave it even after all these years.

SAUNAS

## SAUNAS
*Where All Are Equal*

To sweat is common; to sauna is sacred. Throughout history, since humans have mastered fire, heat has been used to intentionally warm the body, ridding ourselves of disease and ill spirits, creating connection and bonding while fostering a sense of cultural identity and community. In traditional, Indigenous, and folk medicine, sauna has been used as a transformative space, offering those who sit the possibility of finding transcendental states full of euphoric bliss, healing, and profound spiritual growth. Regardless of origin, one thing is true: No one can claim sauna as their own. The art and practice is known by many cultures, but has one intention: profound, healing connection. To one's self, to nature, to community.

Sauna, as we know it today, developed across geographies, evolving in parallel over the last few thousand years. Traced by Finnish author Martti Vuorenjuuri in his little-known 1967 book *Sauna kautta aikojen* (*Sauna Through the Ages*), heat as a form of healing evolved as a sharing of tradition and cultures throughout history. He notes that we should not look for a common origin when it comes to the use of sweat baths because sauna cultures across Europe, Oceania, Africa, and the Americas appear to have developed independently in different regions at different points in time. Of course, many of these traditions became interconnected, playing a major role in what we now recognize as old sauna culture.

It's important to note that the sweat bath cultures of the Muslim world and the Indigenous cultures of the Americas and Africa; the rise of the "great sauna culture" of the Middle Ages in central and western Europe; the *sentōs* of Japan; the *hanjeungmak* of Korea; and the deeply culturally identifiable traditions of Finland, Russia, and northern Europe are all uniquely distinct, but undeniably interwoven. To sauna and to seek heat is universally human.

As enduring then as sweat bath culture is now, for many, saunas have never been just rooms—they have always been a way of life. Places where all are equal and all are welcome. No matter your background or where you come from, saunas are the places in which we come together. They are where life happens and community grows. For the Finns and Estonians, this often meant everything from birth to death happened around—and in—the sauna.

But saunas are also fundamentally about health. From Egypt's rich tradition of medicinal heat therapy to Ayurveda's use of steam chambers and hot stones in India, to the use of herbal sauna therapy in Laos, saunas have always held an important space in medicine as well as traditional healing modalities.

Today, science is embracing what generations have always known, conducting studies that place hard data behind the experiential knowledge we have had forever. In fact, a study published by *Mayo Clinic Proceedings* suggests that "sauna bathing, an activity used for the purposes of pleasure, wellness, and relaxation, is linked to a remarkable array of health benefits" including cardiovascular health, mental health, hormonal balance, inflammation, neurogenesis, attention span, and depression.

The allure of sauna may be that we are blueprinted for relationships, and sauna offers the opportunity to connect, to be vulnerable, and to be incredibly human. To be sure, the ritual and experience of sauna is challenging, but is also a gift.

## The Health Benefits of Sauna

According to Dr. James DiNicolantonio, author of *The Longevity Solution*, 30-minute sauna sessions at least four times per week will boost baseline blood volume, increase red blood cell count, lower baseline core body temperature, reduce electrolytes lost in sweat, and increase sweat production to cool the body better during exercise. Saunas also mimic exercise by increasing immune cells, heart rate, and insulin sensitivity; improve heart health by increasing blood flow, vascular function, and nitric oxide; reduce the risk of infection and the duration of colds; and provide neuroprotection through neurogenesis and the release of heat shock proteins.

# PROJECT Ö

*Self-Sufficient Island Retreat*

ARCHIPELAGO NATIONAL PARK, FINLAND

Aleksi Hautamäki used to spend summers boating around the islands of Finland. "I found the vastness of the archipelago striking in nature and thought it would be amazing to have a place of my own—preferably a separate island." He and his partner, Milla Selkimäki, spent several years searching for empty islands in Finland, eventually landing on a 5-acre [20,000-square-meter] island that they now call Project Ö—a take on the Swedish word for *island*. Though it feels far away from the rest of the world, their self-sufficient home is only about 20 minutes by boat from the nearest harbor and a 90-minute ride to the nearest shops.

Sitting on the southwest edge of Archipelago National Park, the island's human-made structures are designed to echo the traditional aesthetics of the region and to take up as little space as possible. There are two narrow cabins, each with a covered terrace in the center, allowing for a style of indoor/outdoor living that embraces the long summer days.

Designed with a pared-down aesthetic that keeps the focus on the beauty outside, "the vision was to have all things necessary within as little space as possible, without compromising functionality and comfort," says Aleksi. The cabin and sauna exteriors feature vertical Lunawood Thermowood pine cladding, a nod to the surrounding forest, and roofs covered in felt for a matte appearance that allows the structures to blend into the island.

Tucked in the forest nearby, a traditional yet sustainably designed Finnish sauna features a shower, toilet, and a wood-fired Kota Luosto stove. The stove is equipped with glycol circulation, running a broiler under the benches that heats the sauna as well as the property's water and floors. Each evening, Aleksi and Milla enjoy a dip in the sea and a session in the sauna.

## Vihta *and* Vasta

The *vihta*, or bath broom, is traditionally used more in western Finland, and the *vasta* is used in eastern Finland. This bundle of herbs or twigs is used as a sort of whip to circulate the hot air throughout the sauna and to increase the sauna's heat by smacking the broom against the body. Methods for making these twig brooms are passed down through generations, and people can develop a deep emotional connection to them.

According to folklore, here are the uses for each type of plant used to make Finnish bath brooms:

**Birch:** The king of sauna whisks, believed to symbolize virginity

**Oak:** Durable and great for allergies, as it is odorless

**Juniper:** Promotes superficial blood circulation

**Aspen:** For rheumatism and joint pain

**Rowan:** Treats oily skin

**Linden:** Treats sensitive skin and soothes the skin

**Eucalyptus:** Anti-inflammatory and antiseptic

**Alder:** Helps heal wounds

**Pine and Spruce:** Treat a sore back

**Nettle:** Gets rid of toxins

**Black Currant:** Used mainly for its aroma

"We see sauna as a place to stop, observe, and reflect after a usually busy day. It's an important routine, which is why the location and direction were carefully planned," says Aleksi. Sitting atop the island, with a full 180° panoramic view of the sea, the sauna's style and proportions are not typical for traditional Finnish saunas. "For us, the height of the sauna is intentional. With more air above, the steam from the stove falls more calmly, which makes the heat more enjoyable."

The newest addition to the island is a natural pond set into the rock. "We cleared the pit of all the organic material it had gathered in the last 10,000 years from the last ice age," says Aleksi. Here, they smoothed the bottom and connected the pool to the stove, allowing hot seawater to circulate and heat the natural tub to a comfortable 95°F to 104°C [35°C to 40°C].

TRADITION

## Finnish Sauna

Saunas are a fundamental part of life in Finland, which is the sauna's literal and proverbial homeland. In a country with an estimated five million people and three million saunas, most Finns take at least one sauna a week. All aspects of Finnish life have traditionally taken place in the sauna—from births, deaths, and marriages to politics, business, and socializing—and it is prized for its ability to soften the harsh climate, boost immunity, relieve aches and pains, alleviate depression, and detoxify the body.

While Finnish saunas are usually dry saunas, they are known for the practice of *löyly*—pouring water over the hot coals to create steam—and for the herb or twig bunches people beat themselves with to increase their blood circulation.

*Advice from a Sauna Master*

"The sauna needs to be sufficiently hot to generate 'good steam.' It's hard to describe, but you know when it's right. If the rocks are too hot, the water sizzles too fast and you don't get maximum steam generation. The aroma of the sauna matters—like knowing how to properly use spices in cooking. Be sure to use *veniki* that have been soaked in water for hours so the leaves generate their own steam as they pass through the hot air."

—EKIN BALCIOĞLU, COFOUNDER OF *HAMAM* MAGAZINE

# PANORAMA GLASS LODGE

*In the Icelandic Highlands*

HELLA, ICELAND

Created after appearing to its owner in a dream, the Panorama Glass Lodge offers direct views of the active volcano Hekla, the northern lights, the midnight sun, a beautiful river, and the Icelandic highlands—all from the comfort of your bed. Inspired by the simple, rugged beauty of Scandinavian houses, the property consists of four lodges and two saunas completely immersed in nature.

"Saunas are very important to us locals. We think it is important for body health and mental health, as well as a way to deeply relax and unwind," says co-owner Sabrina Dedler. In Iceland, a country that embraces cold winds and freezing temperatures, "we are able to find a greater balance of health by incorporating sauna."

For the full experience, Sabrina recommends two to three continuous sauna sessions of 10 minutes each, with a 5- to 10-minute break between to relax outdoors in the cold air or to have a "super refreshing" outdoor cold shower.

"Wherever you go in Iceland, the most amazing landscape is just around each corner. Fresh air, the ocean, thousands of waterfalls. With such unpolluted air, it is mesmerizing to watch the sunsets and sunrises," says Sabrina.

With so much geothermal activity, it invites the question: Why? Iceland has some of the world's most active tectonic plate movement, allowing the underground geothermal waters to spring up all over the country, making the raw, untouched landscape even more surreal and visceral.

# SWEDANA
*A Traditional Ayurvedic Cleansing Practice*

Ayurveda is a healing practice with roots in India, aimed at longevity and balancing the needs of the mind, body, and spirit. Instead of treating disease, a tenet of Western medicine, Ayurveda works to balance the three energies, or *doshas*, present in the body—*vata, pitta,* and *kapha*—as well as the five basic universal elements present in everyone—space, air, fire, water, and earth.

As a way to purify and cleanse the body, *swedana* or *svedana* is used to reestablish a balance between the *doshas.* Steam-box *swedana* is the most common. Using an herbal infusion to induce steam, patients sit inside a wooden box for about 30 minutes, depending on the treatment. As the sweat glands are stimulated, toxins are eliminated from the body, stimulating circulation.

A critical preparation for the cleansing treatments of *shodhana* or *panchakarma, swedana* is often used after *snehana,* an oil massage, as a pre-cleansing procedure. As the oil massage moves toxins toward the gastrointestinal tract, it also makes superficial tissues soft and supple, relieving stress and nourishing the nervous system. Given daily for three to seven days, the massage is immediately followed by a sweat. The herbal concoction used to create steam will change based on what doshas are out of order, but it may include chamomile, lavender, laurel, eucalyptus, rosemary, or lemongrass.

Some of the benefits of a steam bath include easing stiffness, bringing lightness and softness to the body, releasing metabolic waste, improving digestion, clearing bodily ducts and channels, and eliminating pain.

# TEMAZCAL
*A Low-Heat Sweat Lodge*

Deeply transformative, spiritual, and intentional, *temazcales* have been around for more than a thousand years and originated with the Indigenous peoples of Mesoamerica. The Nahuatl word *temāzcalli,* which means "house of heat," is at the root of its modern name.

A *temazcal* structure traditionally consists of a dome-shaped hut made of clay or stone that, according to legend, represents the earth's belly button. Though *temazcal* ceremonies vary greatly based on territory and tradition, ceremonies that are kept today often symbolize spiritual rebirth and help bring about spiritual healing. To raise the internal temperature of the structure, heated volcanic rocks are placed in the center of the hut, and the space is then filled with the rhythm of drumming and chants as people throw water on the stones. Radiating heat more like an oven than a sauna, the *temazcal* experience illustrates the force and power of nature.

Led by *temazcaleras,* or guides, curanderas, healers, or grandmothers who steward the tradition, the *temazcal* ceremony takes participants through four *puertas,* or portals, of purification—earth, wind, fire, and water—and lasts around two hours. It is often followed by a shower or a cleansing swim in the ocean.

# SWEAT LODGES
*A Spiritual Renewal*

A sacred purification ceremony practiced by many North American Indigenous tribes, a "sweat" is a spiritual tradition that "plays a significant role in the lives of Indigenous communities in their efforts to bring about personal and social healing and commitment to collective values," according to the Lakota Lodge and Harvard University's Pluralism Project. Each tribe has a traditional, unique sweat, which varies according to the historic era, cultural group, and ritual leader. Often, a sweat will include preparing the structure, heating the stones until they are red-hot, bringing them into the darkened chamber, and pouring water or aromatic herbal teas over them as participants sit, chant, pray, and sing.

While the guidelines and experiences vary from lodge to lodge, *inipi*, which means "to live again," is the Lakota spiritual purification ceremony of rebirth, rejuvenation, and awakening. For other tribes, the sweat lodge may represent the womb of Mother Earth, serving as a sacred space for participants to ask for healing, a vision, thanks, or anything else they need on their journey.

The sweat lodge structure is imbued with sacred meaning and power. For the Lakota people, the dome, which is about 4 or 5 feet [1.2 or 1.5 meters] high, consists of a lashed tent of bent willows, which are covered in blankets, hides, or tarps to hold in the heat. The sweat process is elaborate and done with careful preparation and prayer. Inside, the leader respectfully works with the essential elements of water, fire, air, and earth to purify the participants on all levels. The ceremony consists of four "doors," or rounds, each representing one of the four directions, and can last anywhere from two to three hours.

# SAUNA RANCO

*Timber–Clad Sauna*

**LOS LAGOS REGION, CHILE**

Perched atop a granite rock, nestled among the cypresses, sits Sauna Ranco—a simple, beautiful refuge deep in the heart of southern Chile. The intense and raw Los Lagos Region is known for its brutally harsh climate, stunning landscape, and intimate connection to the natural world. Designed by the Chilean architecture practice Panorama, Sauna Ranco blends into the trees and rocks as a quiet conversation and meditative hideaway with private, lakeside views.

The structure of the sauna is a rectangle broken into three rooms—a covered terrace, a changing room, and the sauna itself—all connected by a continuous walkway. Each space is purposefully rotated away from the others, creating a sense of solitude and framing intentional views of the landscape. Wrapped in oak to protect against the elements, the inside is clad in Alamo cottonwood, using light and lines to draw the experience both inward and outward.

Sauna Ranco is heated by a wood-burning stove and sits atop steel supports as part of an environmentally sensitive design that minimally impacts its surroundings by creating a small footprint on the landscape.

# STEDSANS FARM & RESTAURANT

*A Nature Retreat in the Swedish Forest*

**HYLTEBRUK, SWEDEN**

Tucked away in a Swedish forest by a lake sits Stedsans, Danish for "sense of place/direction." Stedsans is a farm and restaurant founded by Mette Helbæk and Flemming Schiøtt Hansen, Danish chefs from Copenhagen who longed for time in nature and a way to share it with the world.

This wooded refuge, a few hours from any city, is an ode to nature, a fairy tale come true. With an on-site vegetable and medicinal garden, cozy cabins, baths, an open-air dining room, and a floating sauna, it's a retreat designed for a lifestyle that brings guests back in sync with the rhythms of nature, slowing down and connecting to the world around them.

Holistic and wild, Stedsans encourages as much presence and interaction with nature as possible. From foraging trips and forest bathing to body therapy, yoga, breathwork, and music, it's an immersive, celebratory feast for the senses.

The lake is central to the Stedsans experience, all year long. In winter, guests enjoy a hot sauna and then jump into the cold waters through a hole cut in the ice. In summer, they lounge with coffee on the deck, enjoying the beautiful lake as a space to take in the sunset or for late-night swimming beneath the summer sky.

Mette shares that while they do not have any organized sauna rituals for guests, she makes homemade sauna oils with different properties and intentions, encouraging people to invent their own. "I often use lavender oil for relaxation, lemon oil for new energy, pine oil for connecting with the forest, and so on. I also like to drink warm herbal tea in the sauna for the full experience of soaking up the healing energies of nature on both the inside and outside of the body, as well as the mind."

For Mette, sauna is best experienced in combination with a cool lake, relaxing an overworked body and mind. "It's a very effective, side-effect–free antidepressant. Like magic, basically."

"In the mornings, I sit sauna and then go in the water a few times. Then I am ready to start the day with a whole new sense of being connected to all there is. After all, we are nature and nature is us."

For the design, Mette and Flemming went to local architects Laurids Bager and Emilie Kjær. Designed to be slightly larger than their previous one, this floating sauna is about 124 square feet [11.5 square meters] and the deck is 377 square feet [35 square meters]. It can comfortably seat between ten and twelve people, but Mette says they have had up to twenty.

The concept was to create "a sacred bathing island . . . a place where you feel like you are sitting outside, almost on the lake, and the movement of the sun is the only thing telling you that time is not standing still," says Laurids. By drawing the outside in and blurring the lines between a life lived inside and one lived in harmony with nature, Flemming and Mette were extremely intentional when considering how to place something in such a delicate setting as the Swedish forest. As Laurids notes, "It is a task that requires simplicity and humbleness."

# CEDAR + STONE NORDIC SAUNA

*Sauna Is a Verb*

DULUTH, MINNESOTA, UNITED STATES

As a proponent of sauna culture in every form, Justin Juntunen, owner of Cedar + Stone Nordic Sauna company, believes that modern life does not have to be as hurried or as stressful as it has become. For him, the simple practice of *hot, cold, rest, rehydrate, repeat* is the antidote to stress and the equation for living a happier, healthier life.

Founded in Duluth, Minnesota (known as the "Sauna Capital of North America" with a century-long history of community sauna tradition), Cedar + Stone offers private, guided sauna experiences as well as community sauna sessions on the shores of Lake Superior. Justin's mission is to share the gift of sauna with his community, as he believes sauna teaches us to overcome challenges: "For me, sauna is a verb and it's an experience to share."

"We know that great sauna starts with great heat," says Justin. "The stove is the heart of the sauna, and sitting sauna is something that should be looked forward to." The tradition of building a cedar sauna in every home or cabin he lives in is one passed on to him from his father, and his family before him, who immigrated from the forests of Finland in the 1880s.

Having stewarded his family's 150-year-old sauna tradition, Justin has made it Cedar + Stone's goal to share his cultural treasure with more people. "What my family has known for centuries is now being backed by science and research."

"One of the joys of sauna is that it's available to so many types of people."
—JUSTIN JUNTUNEN

# OL JOGI WILDLIFE CONSERVANCY
## LAIKIPIA, KENYA

A 58,000-acre [235-square-kilometer] private wildlife conservancy in Laikipia, Kenya, Ol Jogi—named after a local bush—uses tourism to support their widespread conservation efforts. While they offer a Moroccan-style hammam, complete with steam room and sauna, the most enchanting aspect of the untouched property is the opportunity to completely immerse oneself in nature, bearing witness to the unparalleled density and diversity of the wildlife that roams the land.

# HOUSE OF THE WEEDY SEADRAGON

**PIRATES BAY, TASMANIA, AUSTRALIA**

"Rugged and wild, Tasmania is beautiful year-round, and we wanted to use our shack in every season," say co-owners and sisters Lara McCartney and Clair Peachey. "As winters can be cold, the sauna provides a warm, peaceful cocoon; it's a beautiful way to enjoy the weather and storms that roll in over the Tasman Peninsula from across the Tasman Sea. From the sauna, you can watch the tuna boats returning with their catch, humpback whales coming home with their calves, and countless seabirds swarming."

# WHITECAP ALPINE SAUNA

*A Private Backcountry Hideaway*

**PEMBERTON, BRITISH COLUMBIA, CANADA**

In the far backcountry of Canada's South Chilcotin Mountains, just north of Whistler, Whitecap Alpine lodge sits at 6,000 feet [1,830 meters] above sea level, a 20-minute helicopter ride from the nearest airport. Needless to say, it's far away from most things and happy for it.

About 1.5 miles [2.4 kilometers] from the lodge, with an elevation gain of 433 feet [132 meters], the wood-burning sauna is perched atop a boulder on the shoreline of a high alpine glacial lake. When owner Ron Andrews's son Lars Andrews had two large windows left over from a build, he consulted with a local contractor about designing an incredibly private, low-impact sauna. Lars presented his concept: to create "a focal point and [give] purpose to the experience of traveling through the mountains. A place that gives a reason to pause and take in the surroundings [while immersing] oneself in the environment."

Conscious of its impact, the sauna is built from untreated cedar in honor of the surrounding forest (it will eventually fade to blend even further into the environment), sits on four small footings attached to the boulder, and is surrounded completely by water, providing a natural cold plunge that can be accessed by a dock.

Since 1972 the lodge has taken hikers and skiers through McGillivray Pass, and the sauna is one of its newest features, offering alpine flowers, high peaks, and lazy days. "It's the perfect way to revive heavy hiking legs," says guide Hayden Robbins.

# THE BANDS

*Scarcity and Creativity Studio of the Oslo School of Architecture and Design*

KLEIVAN, VESTVÅGØY MUNICIPALITY, LOFOTEN, NORWAY

Ninety-five miles [153 kilometers] north of the Arctic Circle, with craggy peaks, open seas, and sheltered bays, sits the dramatic, remote, and lonely archipelago of Lofoten. With an imposing beauty, the islands are part of the Scandinavian Caledonides, a mountain range that stretches from northern Norway all the way to the south, and comprises six principal islands and hundreds of smaller, unpopulated ones. A dominating presence, especially when approached by sea, the islands' sheer cliffs and clear waters have been called home by humans—from Vikings to local fishermen—for thousands of years.

Lofoten's history is rooted in fishing traditions: The migrating Atlantic cod, or *skrei,* that come to the islands to spawn between February and March have been providing a living for the local people for centuries. Charming, idyllic, and positioned at the top of the world, the islands bask in the glow of the northern lights and the midnight sun, with the perpetual smell of salt air and drying fish. It's home to galleries, artisans, craftspeople, and communities conscious of preserving and honoring their traditions.

Within this landscape sits The Bands, a seaside sauna built on a quay in the former fishing village of Kleivan. The sauna was commissioned by the local district to tie together the old with the new, incorporating three historical pre-existing buildings—a fisherman's cottage (Rorbu), a cod liver oil–production building (Trandamperi), and a cod-salting building (Brygge)—with a new structure. A team of students from the Oslo School of Architecture and Design's Scarcity and Creativity Studio conceptualized and oversaw The Bands's four-week construction.

Evoking the rocks below and waves nearby, The Bands gets its name from three ribbon-like, connected wooden bands that echo the angular landscape. Each band folds to form the 969-square-foot [90-square-meter] structure, made up

of several outdoor areas. To the north, the bands emerge from the rocks, offering a hot tub and a cold tub as well as a rest area. Built sensitively within the surrounding environment, the light-filled, 161-square-foot [15-square-meter] sauna features clerestory windows made from translucent plastic and a gabled wall with windows looking out on the nearby mountains. As the bands bend and fold, they continue to form a fish-cleaning station, a picnic terrace, and many places to lounge and rest.

# ÖÖD MIRROR SAUNA

*Disconnect to Reconnect*

**ORIGINATING IN ESTONIA**

*Ööd* means "nights" in Estonian, and the Mirror Sauna was designed for enjoying cozy nights in nature. Compact and practical, this sauna is a haven of tranquility, featuring two fully mirrored glass walls (lined with a UV-blocking, bird-friendly film) and the option for a wood-burning or electric heater. Intentionally designed to blend into its surroundings, the structure of the Mirror Sauna is purposefully simple and harmonious.

"We created ÖÖD because human beings aren't machines," says founders Andreas and Jaak Tiik. "We need at least a small connection to nature in order to feel our best." Having a place to meditate in the warmth, shielded from the weather outside while enjoying the beautiful views, is the goal. By building a small, practical sauna, "we are able to tap into our innate desire—biophilia—to connect with the environment around us. The more we can do that, the more positive impact it has on our well-being."

Driven by an understanding of "disconnecting to connect," brothers Andreas and Jaak believe finding time to slow down, pause, and be fully present is essential. "As Estonians, we know how to appreciate saunas. The warmth gives the whole body and mind full relaxation."

For sauna, the Tiik brothers value simplicity and follow centuries-old Estonian traditions—hot heat, birch bath brooms, and plunging into cool rivers or fresh snow—leaving your body refreshed and invigorated, "plus, it relieves you from all the stress and tension!"

**STYLE**

### Estonian Sauna

"We like to greet the sauna by saying *'tere saun,'* which means *'hello, sauna,'"* says sauna master and enthusiast Adam Rang, cofounder of Estonian Saunas. "For us, sauna is the entire experience, which includes multiple warm-ups and cool-downs. It's not just a hot room or the brief amount of time you spend in there. Sauna is all of it."

For Estonians, sauna is also a social experience. Humans are social creatures, and friendships are one of the strongest indicators of happiness and longevity. Though the experience of sauna has evolved over the years, "one thing that has remained the same across northern Europe is that it's a communal experience," Adam says. "Going to the sauna enables us to connect more deeply with the people around us. In Estonia, we have an old belief that people shouldn't argue on the same day as going to the sauna, and [you] must make up with anyone you've argued with before going inside."

# SHELDON CHALET

*The Most Remote Hotel in the World*

NEAR DENALI, ALASKA, UNITED STATES

Untamed. Raw. "The Last Frontier." Alaska is synonymous with wild beauty and its landscapes demand respect. Here, simple comforts feel like luxuries.

The Sheldon Chalet sits on a lonely outcropping, a 5-acre [20,000-square-meter] nunatak in the Don Sheldon Amphitheater of Denali's Ruth Glacier. As one of the most remote guest-houses in the world—accessible only by bush plane, or on foot by the very bravest of mountaineers willing to risk their lives—the chalet offers views and an experience like no other.

Just south of the chalet, on the same outcropping, is the Historic Mountain House, a small hut built in 1966. It's perched at an elevation of 6,000 feet [1,830 meters], a short distance from the summit of Denali, in the middle of the 6-million-acre [24,280-square-kilometer] park. Because of this extreme setting, the original owner, Roberta Sheldon, used to ask guests if they were "physically fit and mentally flexible" before they made the journey to the hut.

Roberta and her husband, Don Sheldon, a pioneering bush pilot, originally acquired the land in the 1950s as part of the Homestead Act. The couple built the Historic Mountain House and also planned to build a vacation destination on the property, but were unable to realize the dream before Don passed away in 1975. When the couple's children acquired the hut in 2014, they discovered the original 1968 plans for the chalet and, using those plans as a guide, they were able to realize their parents' dream.

With remoteness and accessibility a consideration, all the materials for the chalet and sauna had to be flown in by plane or hung by a sling and helicoptered in. A stunning accomplishment, the five-bedroom chalet and cedar-lined sauna are a well-earned place to watch a solar storm, witnessing the purples, blues, and greens of the aurora with the naked eye. Located 63° north of the equator, the chalet is designed to endure 100°F [56°C] temperature swings, hurricane-force winds, and the incredibly brutal Alaskan climate.

# THE GROTTO SAUNA
## GEORGIAN BAY, ONTARIO, CANADA

Sculpted and sensual, the Grotto Sauna is hidden in plain sight, nestled on a cliff's edge of Ontario's Georgian Bay. Though the exterior reflects the rugged and extreme landscape of northern Canada, the interior offers glowing warmth and a construction that feels like undulating waves.

The architecture studio Partisans designed the Grotto Sauna as an architectural story exploring escape and refuge that transports visitors to an otherworldly sanctum. The outside was treated in the traditional Japanese method of *shou sugi ban*, when wood is charred to endure the weather. Inside, the space glows with warm, golden tones and features expansive, west-facing windows that allow visitors to enjoy sunsets over the bay. Evoking the intimacy found in Italian grottos, this 800-square-foot [74-square-meter] private structure is warmed by an electric heater and can seat twelve people.

# NIMMO BAY

*Experience Nature by Being Part of It*

GREAT BEAR RAINFOREST, BRITISH COLUMBIA, CANADA

Accessible only by air and sea, Nimmo Bay resort is a truly remote experience—and getting there is part of the adventure. This Finnish-style yellow cedar sanctuary is situated in Little Nimmo Bay, in the heart of the Great Bear Rainforest in British Columbia. Inspired by the ethos of nurture-meets-nature, Nimmo Bay encourages guests to experience their surroundings by jumping into the cool ocean waters, breathing in the fresh air, and walking through the dense forest to a hidden cascading waterfall.

At Nimmo Bay, guests are given time and space to reflect, relax, and reconnect with nature. By tuning into the rhythms of their surroundings and having experiences that make it easy to embrace the wisdom of the ocean and forest without any distraction, guests can truly escape.

The intimate family-owned resort is run by owner-operator Fraser Murray, who grew up on the waters of the bay. The Murrays have been rooted in the wilderness and inspired by the land since 1980, when Craig and Deborah Murray decided, with their young family in tow, to create a new, nature-based life for themselves. Today, their eldest son, Fraser, and his wife, Becky, continue to welcome into their wild backyard all those in search of reconnection and adventure.

From the beginning, the Murray family has strived to realize and share their dream of living off the land, while minimizing their footprint on the environment. Their deep respect for the wilderness around them underscores their belief that spending time in nature feels like coming home. "Not only does it provide visual beauty and gentle stimuli," says Fraser, "but it is a wonderful way of awakening the senses and lifting your spirits with a real, lasting effect. Nature is medicine—ultimately renewing our overall sense of health and vitality."

For Fraser, adding a floating sauna seemed like an obvious choice. Designed and built by a small team including a few friends, the sauna can be reached by boat, kayak, or stand-up paddleboard.

In addition to the sauna, there are two cedar-sided hot tubs located next to the waterfall that runs through the heart of the property. Surrounded by lush rain forests, Nimmo Bay guests can immerse themselves in the healing scents and sounds of the water and woods, while feeling the refreshing spray of the waterfall.

## "We don't recommend any rituals, just to let nature be your guide."

—CAITLIN HEDLEY, NIMMO BAY

The Murrays believe the healing effects of water, like our connection to nature, is ancient. According to Fraser, "[Whether] near, in, on, or under, water has a spiritually restorative effect. It inspires reflection with its constant ebb and flow, the tide gently reminding us of patterns found in nature." From plunges to forest bathing under a green canopy of therapeutic foliage, Nimmo Bay guests are encouraged to embark on walking meditations and hikes, embracing the tranquil silence and beauty of the woods.

# DRIFTWOOD SAUNA CLUB
*A Low-Impact Traveling Sauna*
NORTHERN CALIFORNIA COASTAL MOUNTAINS, UNITED STATES

This custom-designed, hand-built mobile cedar sauna goes wherever creators Ali Hartwig and Whitney Bulterman's curiosity takes them—or wherever it is needed along the California coast. "For us, sauna is about cultivating connection and bliss," say Whitney and Ali. For them, creating the Driftwood Sauna Club was about making a beautiful oasis that they could share and give back to the people they have met, and will meet, along the way.

With an interior of pure, crisp cedar, Driftwood has soft lighting and deep, relaxing heat and is about fostering a mental and energetic safe space. "The magic of the sauna is that it is whatever you bring in there," says Whitney. "As many places we turn to to unwind demand that we consume or do something, sauna offers the opportunity to counteract the pace of modern society by cultivating a space where you don't have to do anything but sweat out whatever isn't serving you."

Ali and Whitney are inspired by the way Driftwood has been used as an alternative location for a book club, as a luxurious outdoor spa, and as a new-moon ritual space. "It's like having your own personal clubhouse," Ali says.

They recommend that guests who are sitting in the sauna listen to their bodies, allowing the soft heat to envelop them. "We think there's a misconception that there is some kind of competition about who can stay in the longest. We recommend enjoying it in 10- to 20-minute cycles," say Whitney and Ali. A cold plunge is a must after the final round.

# HORSEBOX SAUNA AT INSHRIACH HOUSE

AVIEMORE, SCOTTISH HIGHLANDS, SCOTLAND

The Horsebox Sauna is, quite literally, a recycled horse box and army trailer, lined with wood and outfitted with a wood-burning stove. It is located on the 200-acre [0.8-square-kilometer] private highland estate of Inshriach House. The sauna sits about 1 mile [1.6 kilometers] from the main house, among the woods and pastures, bordered by the natural river, and kept company by a herd of Blackface sheep. Populated by a herd of about 130 black sheep and countless red squirrels, the property also features a small gin distillery, saloon, fire truck converted into a two-person dwelling, log house, shepherd's hut, and small bothy—a basic stone steading usually found in the mountains or wilderness, off the beaten track, where you can take shelter.

# MANSHAUSEN ISLAND

MANSHAUSEN ISLAND, NORWAY

Filled and refreshed by the falling and rising tide, Manshausen Island's seawater pond sits in the middle of the Grøtøy strait, in the far north of Norway. The sauna, which is surrounded by sea cabins and a natural plunge pool, features a large, panoramic window designed to bring in the simplicity of nature. Here, a sauna is an enjoyable and social way to connect and warm up during a long winter. With the auroras and the midnight sun, night saunas and swims are encouraged, featuring underwater lights to make the experience even more magical.

# THE BENEFITS OF SAUNA
*A Link to Longevity*

Bathing in heat, in one form or another, is an ancient practice dating back thousands of years. It has been used for purification, cleansing, and healing across diverse cultures. In recent decades, interest in saunas and heat exposure has gained momentum around the world as studies continue to come out linking saunas to longevity and vitality.

When it comes to the measurable health benefits of sauna, it's important to note that there are many types of sauna—from infrared to steam to dry—and each has their own benefit. In a scientific sense, the term *sauna* is defined as "short-term, passive exposure to extreme heat" and is good for us because this exposure creates a mild hyperthermia that mimics a fever in our bodies. In response, our nervous, cardiovascular, and cytoprotective systems all kick in and work together to help our bodies self-regulate. Essentially, it makes our bodies more resilient to everyday life by continually exposing us to small stresses from which we come back stronger. According to Dr. Rhonda Patrick, a leading researcher and expert in the field of longevity, the sweet spot where sauna use has the greatest benefit in terms of measurable results is when it is used at least four times per week, with a duration of more than 19 minutes.

Of course, the benefits of sauna are not all physical. The other benefits are, arguably, hard to pin down and define. However, when considered as part of a holistic or functional approach to medicine, sauna is seen as a way to not only train the body and mind to face challenges, but also to help make the body more efficient when it comes to re-regulating to find homeostasis.

## Humidity

Saunas are either dry or wet. In a dry sauna, the relative humidity is around 20 percent. *Löyly*, or throwing water on the heater rocks, is practiced in Finland to increase the humidity. Finding the perfect temperature in a sauna takes time, changes according to the day, and is unique for each sauna. However, as a rule of thumb, the temperature of the sauna in Fahrenheit plus the percentage of humidity should equal 200. For example, if the sauna is 170°F [77°C], the humidity should be 30 percent.

In a wet sauna, more commonly called a steam sauna, the humidity will be 50 percent or higher.

To fully appreciate the synergistic benefits of sauna, health-span expert Dr. Molly Maloof says that we have to consider its physical, mental, and social implications. Physically, sauna is a hormetic stressor—it puts the body under a high-heat threshold, challenging it to adapt. "This enhances vagal response," Dr. Maloof says, "helping to strengthen your vagus nerve, aiding your body to go into its rest and digest state ... and a strong vagus nerve has been linked to lower rates of depression, better digestion, overall mood, and health." During sauna, the body's temperature "may rise up to 35.6°F [2°C] degrees," causing vessels vasodilation. It's worth noting that, according to Maloof, "regular sauna bathing improves endothelial function, the function of the inside layer of blood vessels, which has beneficial effects on systemic blood pressure." Additionally, sauna is a phenomenal test of mental fitness. "It asks how you can handle things that are challenging without losing your cool," says Maloof. Socially, sauna is a very communal activity, and "the more we can feel a sense of community and connection, the healthier we are. We have to create habits where we talk, relate, and connect. In sauna, we're naked and vulnerable [but] safe. This is a healthy habit for community because, fundamentally, we need to know we are not alone. Our biggest risk to survival is feeling like we are not part of community—it wreaks havoc on our nervous system."

Sauna has a compounding effect and, when used in tandem with a larger and more comprehensive approach to optimizing health span (the period of our lives when we're most healthy), its benefits are hard to deny. Other factors to consider when it comes to health span are: movement and sleep, not smoking or drinking, close personal relationships, not damaging our metabolism, and living in a healthy environment. Fortunately, sauna seems to make everything better. Studies show that it has a positive impact on nearly every system of the body, and that those who consistently participate in sauna are more balanced, healthier, and happier for it.

As a form of self-care, sauna is an incredible practice and habit. According to Maloof, "By sitting and relaxing, we are taking care of ourselves. We're reducing the stress in our lives, freeing up our capacity to commit to other, more meaningful work and demands." Taking the time to sit sauna is extremely good for us, she says. "Getting our bodies out of a stress response is huge for promoting health span and longevity. Our bodies are always in [an interplay between] *stress* and *capacity*. The more we can reduce our stress, the more capacity we have to create, execute, and connect. Not to mention we live in a polluted world, and sauna is an easy way to help our body not have to work as hard."

STRUCTURE

## Far Infrared Sauna

Traditionally saunas were heated by wood fires, a practice still observed today in many saunas throughout the world. Most modern saunas, however, are heated by electric heaters or, more recently, far infrared heaters. Far infrared saunas use ceramic or metal to emit infrared energy at the same wavelength as sunlight. Far infrared saunas operate at lower temperatures than traditional saunas, closer to 113°F to 140°F [45°C to 60°C], making it possible to stay in them longer.

STRUCTURE

## Barrel Sauna

Resilient and durable, barrel saunas are relatively new, but have proven to be one of the most ideal shapes for outdoor saunas. By nature, they maximize the airspace (not letting hot air sit in the high corners of the sauna, away from human reach). Thought to have originated in Canada, barrel saunas were made with long lengths of wood and notched together, bound with tight straps.

## Smoke Sauna

The earliest saunas involved heating rocks outside in a fire
and then carrying them inside to heat a room. Smoke saunas,
however, keep the fire and rocks inside. Here, the fire heats
the rocks and the room fills with smoke. After a time, the smoke
is released and people enter, using the warm room to sweat.

# HINTERHOUSE SAUNA

*A Space for Slow Living*

**LA CONCEPTION, QUEBEC, CANADA**

Designed to embrace comfort and nature, Hinterhouse Cabin is inspired by Norwegian mountains, Japanese design, and minimalist philosophy. Known for creating spaces where design, architecture, and nature become one, the company Hinter has created a vertically clad, low-profile, indulgent, outdoor forest sauna.

Set atop a hill overlooking the Mont-Tremblant Valley, the sauna sits at the bottom of a winding staircase and features an outdoor shower, changing area, and two hammocks. The minimalist, native white cedar–clad sauna will eventually fade to a silver-gray patina, allowing the structure to disappear even farther into the forest.

The 70-square-foot [6.5-square-meter] sauna draws guests in, asking them to immerse themselves in the landscape while offering the chance to escape and relax. David Dworkind, cofounder of Ménard Dworkind Architecture & Design, the company that designed the property, says the "intention is to create beautiful spaces to [experience] that are hidden in the woods and help people escape from the hustle and bustle of the city to reconnect with nature."

# REFUGIO TERRAZA DE LA TIERRA

SIERRA SUR, OAXACA, MEXICO

The Ben'zaa (Zapotec) people, or "Cloud People," in the southern state of Oaxaca are known to have kept a form of *temazcal* alive through the centuries, tracing their lineage back to the builders of the ancient Beningulaás. At the Refugio Terraza de la Tierra, a small hostel in the mountains, everything has been built with natural materials, working in harmony with the ecology of the region. As the owners of the hostel say, the weather changes nine times a day, "with the wind whispering songs of ancient knowledge," as the owners of the hostel offer traditional *temazcal* ceremonies as well as a hand-built sauna nestled among the hillside.

# SORIA MORIA

*Contemporary Public Sauna Inspired by Folklore*

LAKE BANDAK, DALEN, NORWAY

Part sauna, part art installation, the Soria Moria was originally built as a collaboration between the Telemark Canal Regional Park and the Tokke municipality as part of *Vannvegens Fortellinger*, or *Tales of the Waterway*, a large-scale art project that celebrates the beauty of the Norwegian landscape. The sauna sits like a shingle-clad jewel about 100 miles [161 kilometers] from Oslo on Lake Bandak. Stilted just offshore, in the deeper part of the lake, the sauna is connected to land by a walkway intentionally designed to emphasize the natural shape of the Sigurdsevja inlet.

The Soria Moria is bold and geometric, interpreting the steep and striking mountains behind. A few steps from footpaths and walking trails, sitting on mist-covered water, the public sauna can seat fifteen and can be rented for 2 hours at a time. The structure itself comprises three rooms: the sauna, heated by a Harvia electric sauna oven; a changing room; and a covered bench seating area. One of the most beautiful features of the Soria Moria are the gold shingles scattered across its surface—a nod to the local folklore traditions of the region as well as a reference, according to the designers Feste, "to the obvious contrast which arose between the soft-spoken people of Telemark and the lavish upper-class foreign travelers during the establishment of the nearby Dalen Hotel at the end of the nineteenth century."

# ARCTIC BATH & SPA
*Frozen or Floating, Depending on the Season*
SWEDISH LAPLAND, SWEDEN

Sauna, or *bastu* in Swedish, is a natural way of life for the people of the North. Like the midnight sun or the northern lights, sauna and cold baths are deeply ingrained in everyday life here. Cold plunges, together with a warm sauna, are incredibly invigorating and often credited with building the sort of resilience Swedes are known for. This restorative combination is used to ease sore and aching muscles, help the central nervous system, and reduce the body's inflammatory response.

The Arctic Bath & Spa, located just south of the Arctic Circle, was built as a reminder of the region's heritage, its essential connection to nature, and the overwhelming importance of the forest. Situated on the Lule River, an old transportation route for timber, the main circular building was designed to imitate log jams in the river rapids. Here, the sauna experience is about the connection between mind and body, energy and health, earth and well-being. It's about using all of your senses to feel refreshed, release tension, and expand your awareness.

For the best experience, the hotel spa recommends setting aside at least two hours to enjoy the magic of silence and relaxation.

HOT SPRINGS

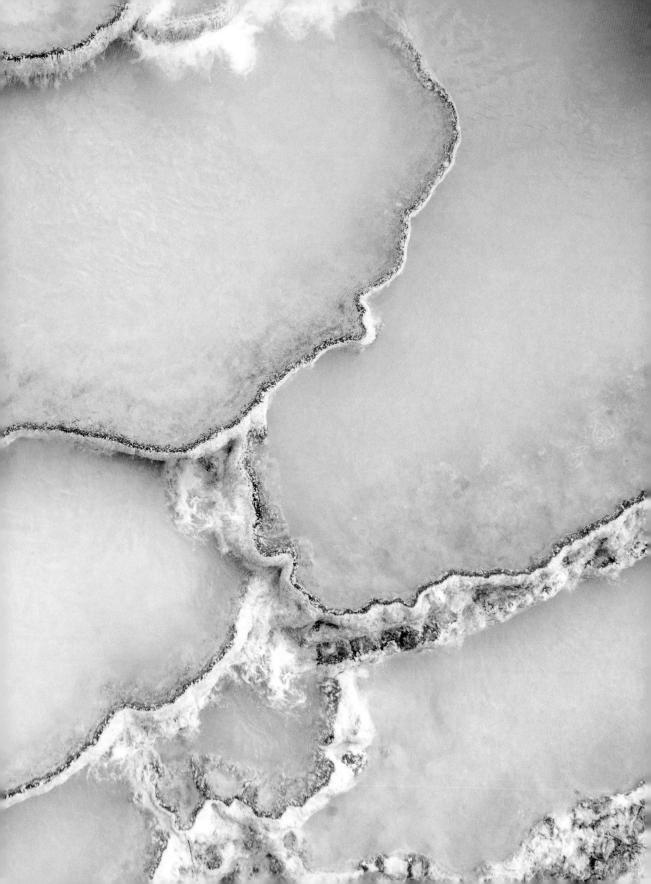

## HOT SPRINGS
*Therapeutic, Healing Waters*

Water pulls life into perspective. Undeniable and interconnected, its energy calibrates us from the inside out, attuning our rhythms to those of nature's. Hot springs, thermal waters, and *aguas calientes* are found on every continent, revered as sacred and held as places of great power. The gift of water is often mythologized and has been associated with goddesses throughout history, connecting us across time to the otherworldly and the divine. It's near water that we hold important ceremonies, celebrating life and death, calling on the power of the natural world to cook, bless, witness, and heal.

With a beauty that does not tire, the poets may be better to ask than scientists when it comes to why we are so drawn to warm waters. Alan Dundes, a professor of anthropology and folklore at the University of California, Berkeley, writes, "One theory along Freudian lines is that bodies of water are female. We are all born from a flood of fluid. There is a security in being drawn back into the womb, and the womb includes water." Of course, there is also the feeling of being held, of cleansing, and the somatic surrender of muscles and tension.

Bathing in natural waters is one of the oldest rituals in the world. In Latin, the phrase *sanitas per aquam* translates to "health through water," an enduring ethos of balneotherapy: The treatment of disease by soaking in mineral waters. Long used in distinct ways by Indigenous peoples, different healing waters (with different mineral properties) have been used to treat various ailments, ranging from the physical to the emotional and spiritual, as well as for purification ceremonies, gatherings, and tribal meetings. Today, throughout Europe and Japan, doctors commonly prescribe hot springs therapy and hydrotherapies as a preventative treatment for many illnesses.

We are creatures made of 60 percent water, so it's no wonder we crave being surrounded by it. Without it, we miss part of ourselves. In the book *Blue Mind: The Surprising Science That Shows How Being Near, In, On, or Under Water Can Make You Happier, Healthier, More Connected, and Better at What You Do*, Dr. Wallace J. Nichols shares that spending time near water is key to "achieving an elevated and sustained happiness." He associates it with what he calls a "blue mind" or "the mildly meditative state we fall into when near, in, on, or under water." This state gives our brains and senses a rest from overstimulation, calming our nervous systems.

Incredibly elemental, hot springs and geothermal waters are psychologically captivating because of their contrast. Here, key natural elements butt up against one another— rocks meet water, hot meets cold, deep within the earth meets the atmospheric sky. It's in these interstitial spaces that two things can be true, and our sense of wonder and magic is ignited as we surrender, releasing gravity and allowing our minds to wander into the space of creativity and possibility.

Out of unconditional respect for our natural lands, all hot springs and thermal waters included here are managed in some way to protect them from overuse. As a reminder, whenever you are visiting any sort of spring, be sure to practice good etiquette, take care of the surrounding environment, speak quietly, and leave it better than you found it.

# ESALEN INSTITUTE
*Where Three Waters Meet & The Healing Arts*
BIG SUR, CALIFORNIA, UNITED STATES

Considered the birthplace of the Human Potential Movement, the iconic Esalen Institute is shrouded in the folk history and back-to-the-land movement of the '60s and '70s. The institute is known for its expansive thinking—having had numerous guest teachers, including famed psychologist Abraham Maslow, best known for his theory on the hierarchy of needs—as well as its countercultural influence, radical approach toward and embrace of the human body, and stewardship of the ancient healing arts. "We are a melting pot of practices, philosophies, and beliefs. Our mantra is 'no one captures the flag,'" says Douglas Drummond, Director for the Healing Arts & Somatics, meaning no one dogma, approach, or belief wins out. "Here, nature maps the human experience."

Esalen is nestled amid 120 acres [0.5 square kilometers] of fertile, redwood-studded Northern California land between the Pacific Ocean and the Coast Ranges. It sits at the intersection of three bodies of water—the Pacific, the natural underground hot springs, and the flowing freshwater from the mountains—on land first settled by the Indigenous Esselen tribe. Long before the institute's founding in 1962, the tribe sent their people to these lands to heal. Here they would go through ceremony, cleansing themselves in the waters and the hot springs.

Esalen's ethos is to trust the process—to surrender to the experience by immersing oneself in the guiding, healing force of nature. Nowhere on the property is that more tangibly embraced than in the sulfur baths, open 24 hours to those staying on the property and from 1 to 3 a.m. to the public for community bathing.

Located just down the hill from the main lodge, the baths are perched above the Pacific, "hanging between sea and sky." Their natural heat comes from the tectonic activity deep within the earth, near the San Andreas fault line, supplying hot water and minerals for the Esalen Institute, Tassajara Zen Mountain Center, Paraiso Springs, and others along the coast. The mineral baths are divided into a silent side and a not-silent side. Both are clothing optional as Esalen believes the practice of being naked and vulnerable together, both physically and mentally, is extremely unifying. "Barriers come down," says Douglas. "We call it 'hot-tub diplomacy,' where conversations happen on the edge, at the edge."

Cultivating contemplation and community, the baths are designed as a refuge. "People bring a range of experiences when they come, and the baths offer support as well as sanctuary," says Douglas. At Esalen, water is held sacred and bathing is both a reflective and celebrated act. For this experience of settling, surrender, and rest, you're advised to arrive without expectation. "We think it's important to have a healthy relationship with the unknown," says Douglas. "Let water be your teacher—all the forms of it. From the ocean to the hot springs, to the sweet water, the fog, the rain, and very much the tears of the people."

Here is a reminder that the nature of practices like sauna, hot water, and cold plunge can be very unsettling and challenging. It is important to remember to never force anything and to approach the experience from a place of receptive, calm intuition.

ABOUT THE THREE WATERS
FOUND AT ESALEN:

## FRESH WATER

Coming from the canyon high above,
the freshwater spring surfaces at Porter
Springs in the Ventana Wilderness

## HOT SPRINGS

Heated by the molten earth below,
the natural mineral hot springs flow at
80 gallons [363 liters] a minute, at a
temperature of 119°F [48.3°C]

## THE PACIFIC OCEAN

The wild Pacific mornings bring thick fog
and evenings bring salt-laden mist

# BAÑOS TERMALES DE CHACAPI

*Abundant Sacred Waters*

COLCA CANYON, PERU

From the volcanic high-desert region of the Andes to the majestic heights of Machu Picchu, Peru has an incredibly diverse landscape, scattered with hot springs (*aguas termales*) from the north to the south. Sometimes a main bathing source for local communities, the waters here range from highly maintained and luxurious to extremely rustic, rural, and wild. As always, it's important to be respectful, aware of local customs, and conscious of your impact on the land—especially when visiting unmanaged pools.

"Visiting hot springs across the country is something we always did as kids," says Peruvian Carlitos Burela. "I remember visiting springs with my *abuelos* like it was yesterday. We'd go to all sorts of local ones, some a few hours from Lima in these quiet Andean towns. There'd be hot springs all along the road, strung along the western slope of the Andes. It was something everyone did, and I'm sure everyone still does."

Located in the Colca Valley, about 186 miles [300 kilometers] north of Arequipa, the Chacapi hot springs are nestled in a dramatic canyon overlooking the Colca River. On one side of the river, bathers can enjoy the older, simpler, and slightly cooler pools. Three newer pools, with hotter water, can be reached via a swinging, cable bridge.

While the Chacapi pools are maintained, a more luxurious experience can be had at the nearby Colca Lodge. They have four private pools, located on the banks of the river, hitting temperatures of up to 176°F [80°C], cleaned throughout the day. The pools themselves have been carefully built with local materials and minimal construction, using stone, earth, and straw.

# AINSWORTH HOT SPRINGS

**KOOTENAY LAKE, BRITISH COLUMBIA, CANADA**

First used by the Ktunaxa First Nations people as a respite
after hunting, fishing, and gathering, these *nupika wu'u*, or
hot mineral waters, were embraced for their healing and
rejuvenating powers. Now the Ainsworth Hot Springs are
owned by the Yaqan Nukiy, the Lower Kootenay Band of the
Ktunaxa people, and they remain Mother Nature's version of
a natural sauna. Sourced from fractures seeping from the
nearby Cody Caves, the mineral water enters the pools at
117°F [47°C] before cooling to an average of 108°F [42°C].

# MATARANKA THERMAL POOLS AND BITTER SPRINGS

MATARANKA, NORTHERN TERRITORY, AUSTRALIA

Boasting 93.2°F [34°C] water filled from the Daly and Georgina basins, the remote Mataranka Thermal Pools and Bitter Springs create a natural lazy river that weaves around the bushland, gently pulling swimmers toward Mataranka Falls. In both springs, the turquoise lagoons are surrounded by an oasis of palm trees and tropical forest, and the resident little red flying fox colony is an entertaining attraction, especially at dusk.

# WAIMANGU VOLCANIC VALLEY

*How the World Began*

ROTORUA, NORTH ISLAND, NEW ZEALAND

Situated within the Pacific Rim of Fire, Rotorua is a hotbed of geothermal activity. The Waimangu Volcanic Valley is the world's youngest geothermal valley—formed by the volcanic eruption of Mount Tarawera in 1886. Renowned for its mud pools, hyperpigmented opaque waters, and natural hot springs, Rotorua is steeped in deep Māori culture. The *tangata whenua*, the Indigenous people of New Zealand, believe in the restorative and spiritual power of the natural world, an idea embodied by *kaitiakitanga*, the Māori concept of guarding over and stewarding the land.

Geothermally, Waimangu (meaning "black water") is a hotbed of activity, featuring the largest hot spring in the world—it is too hot to swim in—with temperatures of 122°F to 140°F [50°C to 60°C]; as well as brilliantly colored microbiology (like the red algae) and intense mineral deposits in the water.

According to Māori mythology, the hot springs came about when a priest, Ngātoroirangi, was caught in a blizzard while climbing Mount Tongariro. He called on his sisters, the fire goddesses Te Pupu and Te Hoata, to come from Hawaiki (their Polynesian home) to relieve his chills. After traveling underwater, the goddesses surfaced on New Zealand's North Island in Rotorua, where the region's hot pools are now found. Today, residents of Rotorua continue to embrace the unique geothermal properties of the area to cook *hāngī*—a traditional way of cooking using an earth oven—in the natural thermal steam and sulfurous water.

# PAMUKKALE
*The Cotton Castle*
DENIZLI, TURKEY

The terraced travertine pools of Pamukkale sit in the southwest Denizli region of Turkey, carrying with them the ancient history of a holy city where emperors soaked and, it's rumored, Cleopatra swam. "Bathing is one of the many practices of letting go," says Ekin Balcıoğlu of *Hamam* magazine. In Turkish culture and around the world, "bathing can be communal or personal," and on some level, it's always profound.

Pamukkale's seventeen pools sit above the Anatolian Plateau, featuring shallow thermal waters that range from 91°F to 212°F [33°C to 100°C]. Heated by subterranean tectonic activity, the water pushes its way through 984 feet [300 meters] of earth, including a layer of limestone that dissolves into the liquid, enriching the bicarbonate and colloidal-iron water with calcium carbonate. As the water evaporates, the calcium carbonate is left behind, creating a gel that eventually petrifies to form travertine, which gives the terraces their iconic white features. This explains the name Pamukkale, which translates to "cotton castle."

The region, which includes the ruins of the Greek holy city of Hierapolis, has been famed for its healing waters since 2 BCE. The springs are steeped in myths and legend, and folklore says the springs used to be where giants did their laundry before disappearing one day and leaving their cotton to dry in the Anatolian sun forever. Others tell tales of a girl throwing herself into the water and emerging beautiful, to be immediately swept up and married by a passing lord, living happily ever after.

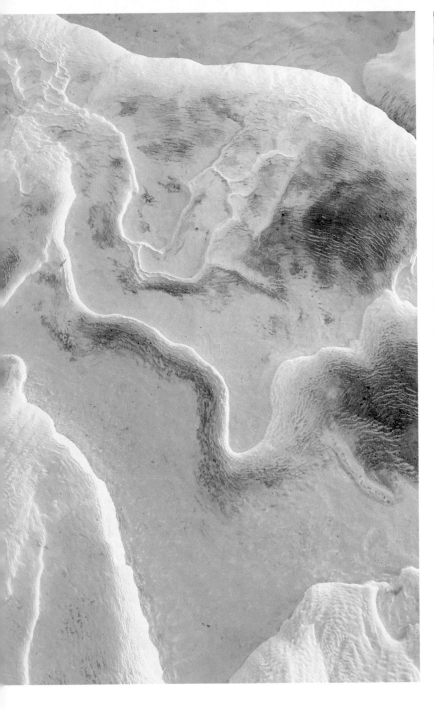

# THE ISLAND OF DOMINICA
*Nature Island*

DOMINICA, EASTERN CARIBBEAN

The youngest of the Caribbean Islands, Dominica is literally built on geothermal activity. With nine active volcanoes—the highest concentration in the world—this lush, immersive rain-forest island boasts 365 rivers and countless ways to experience its truly wild nature.

The names of villages across the island—a vibrant tapestry of European and African cultures—feature a mix of Kalinago, French, and English. Today the common thread across the island for locals and visitors alike is a dedication to preserving and celebrating Dominica's natural landscape and abundant resources. From hiking to diving to soaking in jungle thermal pools to finding adventure around every turn, the experience of Dominica is centered around a commitment to experiencing nature at its most authentic.

Dominica's volcanic origins are dramatically evident across the island—from the steaming wilderness landscapes of the Valley of Desolation to the underwater fumaroles (cracks in the seabed where hot, sulfurous gases escape) in the Champagne Reef to the volcanically heated spas of the Roseau Valley. Dominica's diverse hot springs were formed from a magma layer that lies relatively close to the earth's crust, heating the groundwater with geothermal energy.

Perhaps most impressive, Dominica is also home to the second-largest hot spring in the world: Boiling Lake. It's a 13.5-mile [22-kilometer] round-trip hike up a mountain to experience the nearly 820-foot-wide [250-meter] pool, which reaches temperatures of more than 200°F [93°C]. Because of the high geothermal activity here, it is strongly recommended to use a guide for this hike to know where it is safe to walk.

In contrast, Dominica is also one of the few places in the world that has cold springs. The Cold Soufrière springs emerge from a volcanic crater within the nearby Morne aux Diables. While the water bubbles and hisses like a hot spring, it is actually cold.

Culturally, the island nation boasts a thriving artistic community. And in addition to the more luxurious retreats and spas, there are a number of local hot-spring experiences that are truly unforgettable, such as the ones below.

### TI KWEN GLO CHO

Creole for "little corner of water," this family-owned local favorite, not far from Roseau in Wotten Waven, features multiple springs and various tubs in the middle of the forest. Enjoy mud baths, a bar, and snacks to pass the time.

### TIA'S HOT SPRINGS

One of the original springs on the island, this no-frills spa offers local flavor mixed with authenticity. Tia's features private pools at the top of the hill and a larger communal pool at the bottom; there are also shaded pools, sunny pools, and pools of varying temperatures.

# TERMAS GEOMÉTRICAS

VILLARRICA NATIONAL PARK, CHILE

In Chile, it is understood that well-being comes from connecting with nature. With a chain of volcanoes spanning the
country, it's no wonder Chile has more than 270 geothermal
pools and springs. For thousands of years, the Indigenous
peoples of the land knew about and enjoyed the healing
waters. Today, Termas Geométricas stands as an example
of what it means to be in harmony with nature. Located in
a native forest along a previously inaccessible ravine, the
approximately sixty springs here are accessible via red
wooden planks built to preserve the native landscape.

# CALDEIRA VELHA

*The Green Island*

SÃO MIGUEL, AZORES, PORTUGAL

Caldeira Velha is located on the north slope of the Fogo Volcano on São Miguel Island, one of the nine volcanic islands of the Macaronesian Azores archipelago off the coast of Portugal. Known as the Green Island, or *Ilha Verde*, São Miguel experiences high geothermal activity with iron-infused waters. Rich in biodiversity and geodiversity, the Azores are beautiful year-round, though there are frequent rains and unpredictable weather patterns.

Tucked deep in the lush, green valleys of a tropical forest, the Caldeira Velha is part of the Caldeira Velha Natural Monument, featuring a tumbling, natural waterfall pool and three large human-made pools—all fed by water from the surrounding valley. (There are other natural pools, but they are blocked off because of their excessively high temperatures.) The bathing pools range in temperature from 75°F to 100°F [24°C to 38°C], overflowing from one to the next. Because of the iron-rich water, it's recommended to wear darker-colored swim suits to avoid stains.

# SKY LAGOON
*At the Edge of the World*
**OUTSIDE REYKJAVIK, ICELAND**

Sitting at the edge of the world, Sky Lagoon embodies intensity, tranquility, and simplicity, embracing the rugged Icelandic landscape while simultaneously creating an experience of quiet luxury. Transformative and rejuvenating, it's both ancient and modern, marrying the old ways with the new.

Sky Lagoon's design was intended to honor Iceland's heritage. The aesthetically striking lagoon was built using sustainable and traditional methods like *Klömbruhleðsla*, or turf wall, taking turf from swampy lands and turning it into tiles layered with volcanic ash. This process makes the tiles extremely resilient to the harsh climate of the island.

For the full Sky Lagoon bathing experience, a seven-step bathing ritual is recommended. Bathers begin by entering the geothermal waters through a cave tunnel, wading through and soaking in the steamy waters surrounded by soaring lava-rock walls and a waterfall. Next, they plunge into cold, glacial waters as an homage to the Snorralaug pool in Reykholt, one of the oldest natural pools in Iceland, used by politician and poet Snorri Sturluson, who is believed to have written some of the world's best accounts of the Vikings. The third step is sauna. Visitors heat up for 10 minutes, enjoying views from the panoramic glass-paned sauna as the warmth opens their pores, removes toxins, and flushes the skin. The fourth step is to walk through a cold and invigorating mist. Fifth, bathers scrub themselves clean, cleansing and exfoliating their entire bodies. Sixth, visitors warm up in a steam sauna, hydrating their skin, breathing deeply and relaxing. And finally, bathers wash it all away with a slow, gentle shower.

**EXPERIENCE**

## *Swimming in Iceland*

To fully experience the breadth and beauty of Iceland, Sabrina Dedler, founder of Panorama Glass Lodge, recommends driving the Ring Road— "don't forget about the Westfjords!"—and taking as many baths as possible. Every little town has its own outdoor swimming pool, and there are numer- ous geothermal hot springs to bathe in. "The local swimming pools are your best and cheapest bet," says Sabrina. "Be prepared to shower completely naked with others—it is common and there is even a shower guard on duty to make sure everyone showers thoroughly. Nudity is no big deal in Iceland, and we're super easy-going about it. The only rule is that everyone needs to wear bottoms while swimming."

# CHENA HOT SPRINGS

**FAIRBANKS NORTH STAR BOROUGH, ALASKA, UNITED STATES**

Native Alaskan and Canadian First Nations peoples have traditionally used dry heat and steam baths as a form of healing, and warm thermal waters are still used for relaxation, healing, and recreation today. Located in an area settled in the early twentieth century by surveyors and homesteaders, Chena Hot Springs has a unique mineral profile consisting of sulfate, chloride, and sodium bicarbonate—a combination very similar to the famous waters of Eastern Europe, but not found anywhere else in North America.

# RÍO NEGRO HOT SPRINGS
## RINCON DE LA VIEJA NATIONAL PARK, GUANACASTE, COSTA RICA

Naturally set along the Río Negro in a dense, tropical dry forest near the Rincon de la Vieja volcano, the Rio Negro hot springs are managed by the Hacienda Guachipelín. Accessible by a short hike (or a longer one along the river) and hanging bridge, the mud baths and ten soaking pools (ranging from 98°F [37°C] to 104°F [40°C]) are the main attractions. Here, the mud is gathered directly from the thermal waters—making it full of volcanic minerals—and has been enjoyed in mud baths for centuries.

# A HOT SPRINGS PRIMER
*Minerals and More*

Warm, healing waters have been revered since the dawn of time by both animals and humans. Hot springs became gathering grounds, giving rise to traditions, lore, ceremonies, and rituals around places where weary bodies could rest, the sick could be healed, and celebrations could be had.

Thermal waters are created when rain and snow seep deep below the earth's surface, first pooling as groundwater before being heated by subsurface magma, which creates steam and hot water. This hot, less dense water is then pushed to the earth's surface by geothermal pressure, breaking through fissures and cracks in the ground. As the water makes its way back to the surface, it moves up through layers of rock and earth, gathering minerals along the way.

A hot spring is classified according to where the water is, what minerals it collects, and how it reveals itself on the surface.

**Sulfur and sulfate springs:** These springs are characterized by the presence of hydrogen sulfide and are easily identified by their rotten-egg smell. They are beneficial for skin, nails, hair, and collagen production. In vapor form, sulfur-rich water has significant antibacterial properties and is often used to treat respiratory conditions and skin ailments.

**Saline or salt springs:** In salt-based springs, sodium, calcium, potassium, and magnesium are the main minerals present. These waters typically have a neutral pH of 7 and are used to release tense muscles, ease joint pain, and treat respiratory and skin conditions. These springs have benefits similar to seawater.

**Bicarbonate of soda springs:** These springs can be identified by the bubbling waters from the carbon dioxide present. Soaking in bicarbonate water improves blood circulation as well as most bodily functions. Bicarbonate springs are highly recommended for individuals with hypertension and nervous system imbalances.

**Radon springs:** In trace amounts, radon helps treat skin diseases, diabetes, neuralgia, rheumatism, arthritis, and gynecological conditions. These springs are enjoyed in Europe, but are not approved in the United States.

### Health Benefits of Minerals in Hot Springs

The benefits of soaking in mineral springs happens through transdermal absorption. Even though the skin is a formidable barrier, it is also permeable and porous, allowing trace amounts of minerals to pass through. Below are some of the minerals found in hot springs and their health benefits. For more, see www.hotspringslocator.com.

#### SULFUR (SULFATE)
Protects against damage from free radicals, is critical in collagen production, prevents inflammation, promotes communication between neurons, and improves metabolism.

#### SILICA
An important part of elastin and collagen, making up bones, blood vessels, and skin. Promotes healthy skin, mineral absorption in bones, and arthritis relief.

#### CALCIUM
Critical for healthy bones; necessary for hormone and enzyme production.

#### SODIUM
Maintains fluid balance, necessary for nerve and muscle function, relieves joint pain, and stimulates the lymphatic system.

#### BICARBONATE
Improves blood circulation, helps to manage hypertension, and neutralizes acidity.

#### BORON
Helps build muscle.

#### MAGNESIUM
Important for nerves and muscles to function properly, relieves tension, and tightens skin.

#### SELENIUM
An antioxidant important for the proper functioning of the thyroid gland.

#### POTASSIUM
Aids in nerve transmission and regulates the body's fluid balance.

#### LITHIUM
Improves overall brain function and helps alleviate depression.

# TERME DI SATURNIA AND CASCATE DEL MULINO
*Bathing Under the Tuscan Sun*
SATURNIA, MAREMMA, ITALY

Just 1.8 miles [3 kilometers] from one another in the Maremma region of Italy, the Terme di Saturnia and Cascate del Mulino are beautiful natural hot springs open year-round. The springs are near an ancient Etruscan necropolis—a large cemetery—in an area once inhabited by preclassical populations of Greeks and, later, Romans.

According to Roman mythology, the springs were born from a fight between Jupiter and Saturn. During the battle, Jupiter's thunderbolt hit the earth and the point of contact opened a portal to the underworld, releasing hot, sulfurous waters.

In truth, the waters come from a geothermal spring that seeps through tectonic plates of Mount Amiata in southern Tuscany. Brimming with minerals like sulfur, carbon, sulfate, and bicarbonate, the waters can reach a temperature of 99.5°F [37.5°C] and are widely believed to have relaxing and rejuvenating powers.

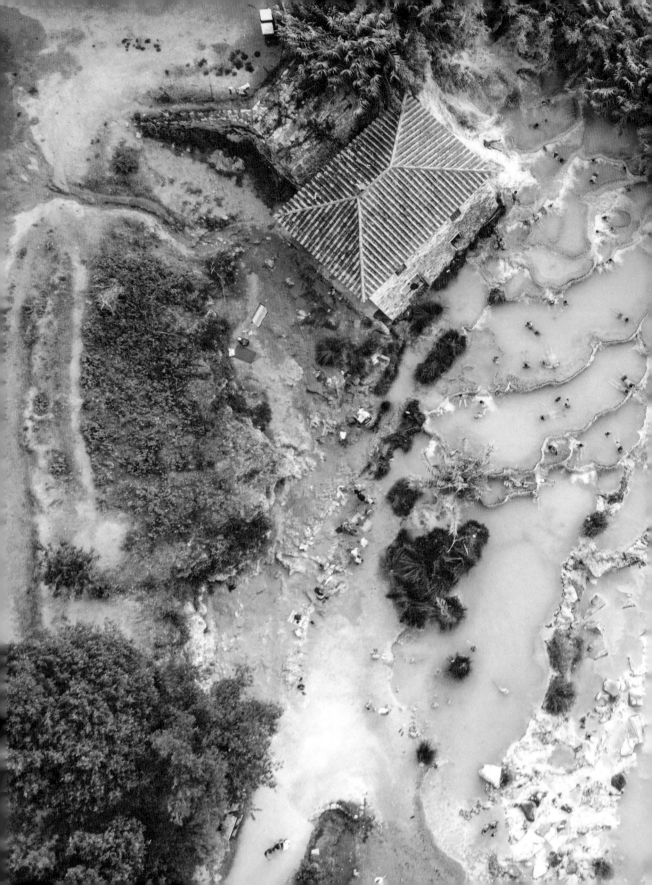

# COLD EXPOSURE
*Embrace the Discomfort*

The history of ice bathing and cold exposure dates back thousands of years, from the ancient Greeks to the Vikings, transcending time and culture to become a ritual now widely practiced across the globe. Longevity researcher and expert Dr. Rhonda Patrick notes that while cold exposure is often used to reduce muscle soreness and promote recovery, regular cold exposure may also improve glucose and lipid metabolism, decrease inflammation, enhance immune function, and improve cognitive performance. The benefits may be linked to hormesis, "a favorable biological response to a mild stressor that triggers mechanisms that provide protection from future, more harmful stressors."

Julian DeSchutter, a teacher and longtime practitioner of cold exposure, shares how to start reaping the benefits of this practice:

> Simply put, cold exposure doesn't have to be anything more than exposing your body to generally uncomfortably cold temperatures ranging from subzero to an upward boundary of 50°F [10°C] for a few minutes at a time. The environmental medicine does the work for you.
>
> To get introduced to cold exposure, start by taking 30-second cold showers in the morning. Not only will these teach you about the power of cold, but they are also invigorating, helping you to feel mentally clearer, more relaxed, and rejuvenated.
>
> As your body adjusts, you can gradually work up to even colder temperatures for a longer duration, gaining more benefit as you do so. You can move from your indoor shower to an at-home ice tub or, our favorite in Canada, a chilly lake or slow-moving stream.
>
> When it comes to cold exposure, there really is no "right way." From cryotherapy to cold showers to an at-home ice bath or forest bathing, all are legitimate. However, cold exposure is not just about jumping in the water and suffering for as long as you can. It's deeper than that—it's about strengthening the relationship and communication between your body, nervous system, and mind.

Cold exposure trains us to control our physical and mental reaction to negative stimuli and, ultimately, gives us an arena to better learn how to control our experience of life.

One of the primary mechanisms that helps us train for the cold is breathing—before, during, and after the cold tub.

Similar to Pranayama (yogic breathing) and Tibetan Tummo ("heat" meditation), there are two stages to breath practice: The first involves taking thirty to forty rapid "power breaths," where you inhale deeply and exhale quickly (almost like you're mimicking hyperventilating). The second stage is retention. This involves taking one deep inhalation, a full exhalation, and then holding your breath for around 10 seconds while clenching all your muscles. These techniques can be quite advanced, and it's best to attempt them only after guided training.

As with anything, cold exposure is not for everyone, and it's crucial to have the proper supervision and training. Health-span and longevity expert Dr. Molly Maloof says that women should not practice it daily, but suggests that everyone practice a combination of heat and cold exposure therapy. Dr. Rhonda Patrick notes that caution should be exercised when alternating between hot and cold environments, such as from sauna to plunge pool, as dramatic changes in blood pressure can occur.

# DUNTON HOT SPRINGS

*Rustic Luxury*

DOLORES, SAN JUAN MOUNTAINS, COLORADO,
UNITED STATES

The 1800s silver-boom ghost town of Dolores has a history all its own. Originally stewarded as the summer hunting grounds of the Ute people, this small alpine valley outpost started as an unincorporated settlement before it was established as a mining camp in 1885, only to be abandoned by 1918. After years as a working cattle ranch and then dude ranch, the property was renovated in 1994, over the course of seven years, as an immersive, luxury retreat with sustainability and healing waters at the forefront.

These exclusive springs seep from deep within the San Juan Mountains, emerging from a north-trending fault line, pouring out calcium bicarbonate–rich waters with a concentration of dissolved iron, manganese, and lithium. Water temperatures range from 85°F to 106°F [29°C to 41°C].

Though the original spring still exists, today there are five different locations across the property to take in the healing waters: the restored nineteenth-century bathhouse, both an indoor and outdoor experience; under the Colorado stars at the source point; in a pool outside the bathhouse; in another pool behind the Dunton Store cabin; and inside the Well House cabin.

# GOLDMYER HOT SPRINGS

*The Old Mine Shaft*

CASCADE MOUNTAINS, WASHINGTON, UNITED STATES

To reach Goldmyer Hot Springs, visitors must drive to the end of a forest road and complete a long hike deep into the woods. The hike in follows the Snoqualmie River upstream, lined with old-growth and second-generation trees draped heavily in moss and boulders hugged by lichen. Just past the meadow and Burntboot Creek, Goldmyer's property begins and the cave, from which water cascades filling nearby pools, is not far away.

The 20-acre [81,000-square-meter] wilderness preserve allows just twenty visitors per day. Managed by the Northwest Wilderness Programs since 1976, the caretakers check in on visitors, turning away anyone who doesn't have a reservation. The goal of the Northwest Wilderness Programs is to allow the ancient forest to continue to heal itself by limiting access.

Minimally developed, the crystal-clear geothermal springs emerge from an old mine shaft, with water steadily flowing at 125°F [52°C]. Visitors can pair their hot immersions with chilling dips in a nearby cold-water pool.

# LAS GRUTAS DE TOLANTONGO AND LA GLORIA

*Box Canyon Hot Springs*

MEZQUITAL VALLEY, HIDALGO, MEXICO

The origins of the name Tolantongo come from the Uto-Aztecan Nahuatl word *Tonaltonko*, meaning "home where it feels warm" or "place where it flows warm." The springs were known locally as *Tonaltongo* before an unfortunate magazine misspelling in the 1970s popularized the wrong name. Today Tolantongo is run by an association of 112 families who own the San Cristobal *ejido*—a type of communal property where the land is run by and for the benefit of the people. Across the valley and a suspension bridge, the La Gloria pools are part of the La Mesa *ejido*.

The box canyon is steep and striking, with walls reaching 1,640 feet [500 meters] high. Heated by the surrounding volcanic mountains, Las Grutas de Tolantongo park is made up of two main caves. The heated underground river flows from the largest cave, following the canyon floor and feeding more than thirty mineral pools throughout the park.

Across the valley at La Gloria, the atmosphere is calmer and quieter. With large pools and tubs nestled into the hillside, temperatures are around 100°F [38°C]. This side of the canyon also features a thermal waterfall, steam cave, and warm river.

# HOT WATER BEACH
## MERCURY BAY, NEW ZEALAND

Located on the northeast shore of
New Zealand's North Island, Hot
Water Beach sits in Mercury Bay,
part of the Coromandel Peninsula,
an area renowned for its beaches,
misty forests, and rich Māori culture.
At Hot Water Beach, just underneath
the sand, deep geothermal springs
bubble up, accessible between high
and low tide. With temperatures
reaching 147°F [64°C], soakers often
dig many holes, finding the right
temperature and soaking until the
tide washes their baths away. (It's
worth noting that there is another "hot
water beach" on the west coast called
Kawhia, which is fed by the underground Te Puia geothermal spring.)

# TERMALES SANTA ROSA DE CABAL
## RISARALDA, COLOMBIA

Located in the region's Coffee Triangle, these volcanic hot springs were first discovered in the early 1940s by a local family and opened to the public shortly thereafter. Including both hot and cold pools, the springs are situated at the base of three neighboring waterfalls. A popular destination for locals and visitors alike, Termales Santa Rosa de Cabal features human-made pools as well as steamy lagoons hidden in the forest, but the main attraction is the Santa Helena waterfall that flows through the property.

# THE BLUE LAGOON

*A Geothermal Wonder*
**GRINDAVÍK, ICELAND**

The Blue Lagoon's geothermal waters are 70 percent ocean water and 30 percent fresh water, enriched with silica, algae, and minerals. According to their website, this is a place "where the powers of science and the wonders of nature create transformative experiences." Used by locals since it was discovered in the 1980s, the lagoon's healing waters are sourced from the Mid-Atlantic Ridge, where tectonic plates are pulling apart, allowing magma to heat the water and create this otherworldly landscape.

Steaming against a black basalt moonscape, the turquoise waters are about 100°F [38°C]. They were originally discovered to have unique healing qualities in the 1980s, when a reservoir formed in the lava fields and curious locals began to swim in it. Since then, the Blue Lagoon's geothermal seawater has been closely studied for its nourishing benefits.

# TERMAS DE CACHEUTA
**MENDOZA, ARGENTINA**

Secluded in a gorge in the Andes, about an hour outside of
Mendoza, lies Termas de Cacheuta. While locals often visit
the nearby Parque de Agua Termal, the fancier and more
full-service experience is at the Termas de Cacheuta spa.
An indulgent, relaxing experience, this series of hot springs
overlooks the wine country and feels like a sunken garden.
Though these hot springs, surrounded by mountains at the
base of the Andes, are not as wild as many other hot springs
in Argentina, they are a beloved experience. Sourced at
142°F [61°C], the pools vary in temperature from 86°F
to 117°F [30°C to 47°C].

# THE PENINSULA HOT SPRINGS
## MORNINGTON PENINSULA, VICTORIA, AUSTRALIA

A short trip from Melbourne, these hot springs have 360° views from hilltop pools over-looking the Mornington Peninsula. Brothers Charles and Richard Davidson founded the springs in 1997. While living in Japan, Charles was inspired by Japanese bathing culture and wondered if a globally inspired outdoor bathing culture could take shape in his home country of Australia. Not surprisingly, it did.

The Peninsula Hot Springs offer mineral-rich waters at a variety of temperatures, from cold plunges to steamy dips. The winding paths and bushy tracks hide pools designed for communal interaction as well as calm and quiet. Set in an idyllic coastal setting, and featuring more than fifty internationally inspired bathing experiences, the bathhouse features a hilltop pool, amphitheater pool, baby barrels, cold plunges, geothermal bathing, body clay, hot and cold therapy, and more.

# MAPLE GROVE HOT SPRINGS

*A Riverfront Restoration Retreat*

THATCHER, IDAHO, UNITED STATES

Maple Grove Hot Springs is an experiential riverfront retreat center that supports personal, community, and ecological wellness, and also happens to have hot springs, according to co-owner Jordan Menzel and Creative Director Jainee Dial.

After physically restoring this cherished but run-down property, Jordan and Jainee realized that it also needed a cultural refurbishment that would be holistic, generative, and enduring. They felt that their approach to this revitalization should be sacred, honoring the deep ties to their community, their neighbors, the local economy, and the fragile ecosystem.

Long before the yurts and solar panels, and before the pioneer homesteaders and eclectic group of hot-spring soakers, this land was home to the Shoshone tribe. "For us, restoring the land and waters meant weaving connections to the Indigenous ties that [our] native predecessors had to these healing waters," says Jordan. "The future depends on how we acknowledge the past and elevate its connection to the present."

After three years of collaborative restoration work, the Maple Grove community feels rooted. They know what it means to be in the business of wellness—Maple Grove is the first hot-springs retreat to become a certified B Corporation, a company that voluntarily meets the highest standards for social and environmental performance. "We want to be connected, for better or worse, to the broader ecosystem, socially and environmentally," Jainee says. "We want to dedicate [our] resources, programming, and storytelling to causes like mental health and suicide prevention, and the creation of the Boa Ogoi Cultural Center [a cultural interpretive center honoring the 400 Shoshone people massacred in January 1863]."

This also means a more deliberate use of the healing waters here. While people come to soak and experience mental and physical well-being from these lithium-rich pools, they also come to grow emotionally and socially. "Growth is not found in comfort. It's not 'found' at all. It's created, and that creation can often be uncomfortable," says Jainee. "As an active retreat center, we focus on fostering a peaceful, predictable, and transformative experience for all who come."

At Maple Grove, Eastern practices of silence are followed, guests are limited, and thoughtful guidelines are given a laid-back Western twist rooted in creative experiences and communal wellness. "We want [your] time at Maple to pose the question, 'What if this experience had the chance to change the way you view both your inner and outer land-scape?'" Jordan says.

"As a culture bombarded with digital stimuli, we often hide from life's quiet moments by retreating to a virtual world of 'anywhere but here, anytime but now, anyone but those near us,'" Jordan says. "We felt it was important to digitally detox on this land. That to truly connect to the natural environment and one another, we have to remove distraction. The results have been profound. Complete strangers connect to one another. Diverse people from all walks of life are embold-ened to interact, ask questions, and converse freely."

The River House guest book greets visitors with this simple statement: "Water, Wildness, Humans, and Spaces. These are our offerings and you are their guest. Welcome."

"We feel like what's going on here will outlast us all," Jainee says. "These waters have risen from deep within the earth for time immemorial, and it takes constant revitalization to keep up. That's why our mission and our intention for this land and these waters is: *May we be well. Within the bodies we inhabit, within the communities we gather, and within this wilderness we steward.*"

## THE ART OF BATHING
*A Practice of Release*

Quintessentially primal, the allure of bathing is in its ability to bring cultures together across history. Humans have ritualistically immersed themselves in water throughout the ages, innately drawn to the liquid element as a way to cleanse, commune, and connect. No matter the form, water as a simple necessity holds a deeply ingrained, and often sacred, place in humans' evolutionary psyche—from bathhouses to private soaking tubs, our collective history is entwined with the culture of bathing.

The earliest-known public baths were built in the Indus Valley around 2500 BCE, in the lost city of Mohenjo-Daro, in present-day Pakistan. Called the "Great Bath," this large pool was made of baked brick and, according to anthropologists, may have been used as a temple. Centuries later, around 300 BCE, Romans adopted the practice of communal bathing, making it an egalitarian staple of society. One part hygienic, one part social, and one part spiritual, public baths became the space around which life happens—and continues to happen—a haven of relaxation, connection, and calm.

Though the world has never seen anything like the bathing culture of ancient Rome again, today the revival of bathhouses and bathing is continuously on the rise. An antidote to an overworked, overstimulated, and often disconnected culture, bathing offers the opportunity to reconnect, slow down, and find purpose in the present—a truth embraced by medicinal practices like Ayurveda and traditional Chinese medicine, where water is used as a balancing force.

However, the traditions of our ancestors are at risk of being forgotten unless they are uncovered, celebrated, and revived. More than just personal, our emotional and physical interactions with the most prevalent substance on the planet have incredible implications for individual, societal, and environmental health—either perpetuating our sense of oneness with the world or our division from it. Not surprisingly, in the *Los Angeles Times* article "Aquatic Attraction: Poets, Pragmatists and Scholars Ponder the Inexplicable Appeal of Being Near Water," psychiatrist Dr. Tom Rusk notes, "There is something extremely basic or primitive about water, [the understanding of which] doesn't require you to be scientific."

Fortunately, there is plenty of scientific backing to support what generations have always known: Bathing is not just good for our emotional and spiritual health, but our physical health, as well. Bathing and the ritualistic practices of bathhouses are widely studied and known to be beneficial for cardiovascular health, skin ailments, post-traumatic stress disorder, depression, anxiety, and more.

From Turkish hammams and Russian *banyas* to Korean *jimjilbangs*, Japanese *onsen*, and bathing in spectacular as well as private places around the world, the common thread throughout is that of connection. Whether to one's self, past, culture, or community, the act of bathing—of immersing oneself in water, or intentionally moving through heated rooms designed to cleanse—takes us out of our heads and into a more somatic, connected state.

Undeniably evocative, inspiring, and universal, the allure of water is as powerful as it is peaceful, and the art of bathing becomes ritual when imbued with intention, transforming it into an act of prayer and focused thought.

### Elements of a Ritual Bath

To take bathing from activity to ritual, all it takes is intention. "Whether your intention is to heal, to feel restored, to release stress, or to simply have a moment to yourself, taking the time is always worth it," says Max Turk of Roots & Crowns Apothecary in Portland, Oregon. Here, Max offers elements to consider adding to a ritual bath:

**Salt:** Salt naturally draws out and clears physical and energetic toxins. You can add Epsom, pink Himalayan, or sea salt to your bath.

**Oils:** Oils can make the water smell good and nourish your skin. Be sure to dilute essential oils to avoid skin irritation and add them to salts before adding to the bath. Try lavender or eucalyptus.

**Botanicals:** From flowers to sprigs and greenery, botanicals add a beautiful, fresh element to a ritual bath. Sprigs of cedar, eucalyptus, or lavender and blossoms of rose, calendula, and marigold are beautiful additions.

**Flower Essence:** Subtle yet powerful, flower essences imprint the healing properties of the flower and transmute it into a bottle. Add a few drops to your bath, absorbing the essence through your whole body.

**Crystals:** Crystals carry different properties, so choose one that aligns with your intention. You can place the crystal in the bath or set it on the edge of the tub. Energetically, it charges the water the same way it would as if placed on your body.

# ONSEN

*A Meditative Soak for Body and Mind*

ORIGINATING IN JAPAN

*Onsen* are Japanese hot springs and often refer to the bathing facilities, both public and private, that surround them. As a volcanic island, Japan's semi-sacred bathing culture is built around the country's unique topography, with approximately 27,300 hot springs and 2,980 *onsen* towns (entire towns dedicated to the *onsen* bathing pools in the area). According to Japanese acupuncturist and natural herbalist Sachiko Tada, water is part of Japanese spirituality and connection.

For Tada, "bathing is like prayer. Soaking is not to be rushed," but rather approached as a time to contemplate nature and to experience *gokuraku*, an experience of divine pleasure in the body.

Buddhist teachings have promoted purification and bathing from as early as 780 CE, and *onsen* are even described in Japan's first history book, written in 700 CE. Tada notes that, with so many accessible springs, people travel to different *onsen* based on the minerals in and qualities of the waters. While *onsen* are easy to find in the countryside, they can also be found in Tokyo, Kyoto, and most city centers.

As integral to Japanese culture as sake and sushi, onsen are informal spiritual spaces, quiet and revered. Leisurely, meditative, and sensual, *onsen* is not meant to be rushed, as Tada says. Whether you go before or after work, for a weekend away, or as a *toujiyu* (a retreat to the hot springs when you're sick and need to rest), *onsen* is about the mind, body, and spirit. It is also about connection. "When I soak with someone, I feel like we are family, connected to the universe," Tada says. "We speak in small voices, with open minds, about any topic."

"For us, *onsen* is 100 percent Japanese, and deeply spiritual. It is about the power of the earth—the water comes from the rivers, oceans, and mountains. When I am having *onsen*, I feel the power and energy of the earth as I soak."

Men and women traditionally bathe separately and completely nude, and only in some *onsen* are tattoos allowed. To show respect for both the waters and other people present, everyone must shower before entering the pools, and ensure that neither their hair nor their towel touches the water. It is important to speak quietly, not run or swim (simply soak), and to be mindful of others and their experience.

"I invite everyone to come and soak in an *onsen*," Tada says. "If you do, you will feel a deep relaxation in the warmth of the water. You will feel connected to the energy of the earth, to your heart, mind, body, and spirit. You will feel that we are all one."

# KUROKAWA ONSEN
## KUMAMOTO PREFECTURE, JAPAN

Kurokawa Onsen is one of the most frequented hot-spring towns among Japanese bathers, but is relatively unknown to Westerners. Located in the mountains of Kumamoto Prefecture, visitors to Kurokawa typically embrace the relaxation and seclusion of the region by staying in a traditional *ryokan*, or inn. For a local treat, *onsen tamago*, or hot-spring eggs, are boiled in the stable thermal waters and sold as street food as a regional delicacy; in Hakone, the eggs are boiled in sulfurous volcanic waters, turning their shells black.

With no hotels or colorful signs, Kurokawa boasts only the pure and simple aesthetics of a traditional Japanese village surrounded by forests, mountains, and calming rivers. Featuring ancient wooden buildings and earth-and-stone stairs, the town is lined with small shops and inns, and bathers shuttle from one *ryokan* to another wearing their *yukatas* (robes) and *geta* (sandals).

# GELLÉRT BATHS
*Art Nouveau Thermal Waters in the City of Spas*
BUDAPEST, HUNGARY

Known as Spa City since 1934, Budapest has an abundance of riches when it comes to its countless fountains of thermal waters. An impressive 18.5 million gallons [70 million liters] of 70°F to 82°F [21°C to 28°C] thermal waters issue daily from the city's 118 naturally occurring springs. In fact, an underground series of springs run next to the Danube River and a network of thermal baths above ground allow access to the city's waters.

Since the thirteenth century the region has been famous for its healing waters, and visiting the hot springs is an integral part of life here. Frequented as often for their health benefits as for the opportunity they provide to catch up, swap stories, and gossip, the baths of Budapest are both a solitary and a social affair.

Of all the baths here, the most famous is the Gellért Baths, known for its Art Nouveau and Art Deco furnishings, artistic mosaics, stained-glass windows, and opulent sculptures. The main allure here is the design of the complex, which features six pools and a glass roof that opens during the summer. The mineral-rich waters pour over multiple layers of glazed ceramic tiles, which also feature mosaics that mark the temperature—104°F [40°C] in one pool, 97°F [36°C] in another. Outside, you can either lie in the cold pools or play in the wave pool that has been in continuous operation since 1924.

# A BATH HOUSE

*The Ancient Made Modern*

WILLIAMSBURG, BROOKLYN, NEW YORK, UNITED STATES

The business model for A Bath House is at least 5,000 years old—or even older if you consider that humans have always been drawn to hot springs and heat rituals. In this 1800s Brooklyn soda factory, the experience of communal bathing as a foundational, borderline-primal human experience is not intended to be improved upon—merely modernized and made mainstream.

A Bath House owner Jason Goodman has embraced a "no rules" philosophy of what a bathhouse can be. Seeking to design a deeply human social experience that forgoes the isolating, performative relaxation of luxury spas, he cherry-picked the bathing elements he loved most from decades of firsthand bathhouse experiences, drawing on different cultures around the world and presenting them in a clean, modern way, focusing on modalities that have stood the test of time.

"Water is always the center of
 life, in any environment."

—JASON GOODMAN, OWNER

A Bath House features dry and tropical saunas, a starlight steam room, three thermal pools, and heated marble hammams. The dry, or Scandinavian-style, sauna runs between 175°F and 190°F [79°C and 88°C]. The tropical sauna is 185°F [85°C], but with its high humidity, it feels more like 200°F [93°C]. The thermal pools range from hot (104°F [40°C]) to cold (52°F [11°C]) to thermoneutral (94°F [34°C]).

T
H
E
R
M
A
L

"A Bath House is about being humans, being the best versions of ourselves that we can be."

—JASON GOODMAN

## A Bath House Bathing Ritual

According to owner Jason Goodman of A Bath House in Brooklyn, there is no wrong way to do a bathhouse circuit, but different approaches are followed for different outcomes. Some circuits optimize post-athletic recovery, or are for injury, detoxification, or just general health and longevity. This is Jason's general health circuit, to be done four times a week:

1.  Start with the steam room to open up a little. Untimed duration, with a short cool-off afterward.

2.  Take a dry sauna for 15 to 25 minutes at 175°F [80°C] or hotter. No breaks; just push through.

3.  Directly from the sauna, go to the cold pool for a 3-minute plunge. Catch your breath!

4.  Rest. Sit on a bench with the cold for a few minutes after the pool.

5.  After that, do whatever you want, and mix it up!

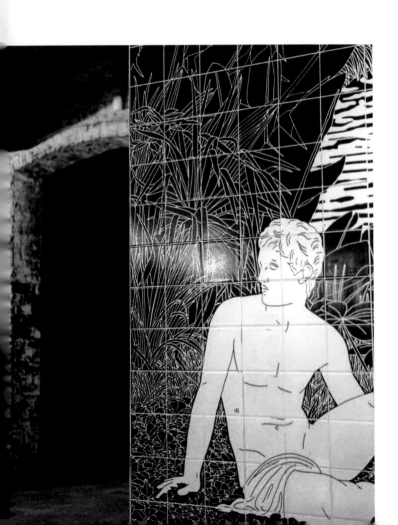

# SANDUNÓVSKIE BANYI

MOSCOW, RUSSIA

In a country where *banya*, a traditional Russian steam bath, is a way of life, Sandunóvskie (Sanduny) is Russia's oldest and most luxurious public bathhouse. With separate areas for men and women—the most opulent being on the men's side—this *banya* features traditional steam rooms, buckets of cold water, plunges, and *veniki* (oak leaf branches) for the *platza* massage.

## *Russian* Banya

# "In the *banya*, all are equal."

—RUSSIAN PROVERB

In Russia, *banyas* are a foundational and inextricable part of the culture, and where the business of life is conducted. To protect themselves from the extreme heat in these steam-filled bathhouses, visitors wear *chapka*, or felt hats. Loud, social, and intimate, *banyas* are used as much for community as for health. Perhaps the most famous aspect of the *banyas* is the *veniki*, or birch bundles, which are dipped in icy water and used to beat bathers, stimulating their pores.

*S'legkim parom!* ("With light steam," the linguistic equivalent of "*bon appétit!*" for baths.)

# BAD GASTEIN
*A Fairytale in the Mountains*
BAD GASTEIN, AUSTRIA

Once an escape for the eccentric creatives and visionaries of Europe, and once known as the Fountain of Youth, Bad Gastein has once again become a spa-lover's paradise. This famed spa town, cut into a gorge and nestled among the Austrian Alps, is known for its radon-rich healing waters that once healed emperors and empresses who came here to hike, soak in the curative baths, and take in the dramatic landscape. Enchanting Belle Époque hotels are dotted throughout the village, carving up the steep mountainside around the 656-foot-long [200-meter] waterfall in the center of town.

Bad Gastein's healing thermal waters are easily accessed through a hotel's private spas, but the most striking feature of the village is the Brutalist architecture of the Felsentherme spa. This sprawling structure, featuring indoor and outdoor thermal baths, is frequented by locals, who walk the winding, mountain streets in their bathrobes to reach the waters.

Bad Gastein's mineral-rich healing waters come from eighteen springs at the base of the Hohe Tauern mountains, the end of the springs' 3,000-year journey through the alpine rock layers. Bubbling to the surface enriched with minerals, the waters are believed to revitalize the body, stimulate circulation, promote relaxation, and offer a state of deep mindfulness.

Nadin Brendel, a resident of the tiny mountain village, says, "My favorite Bad Gastein morning ritual is quietly soaking and floating in Bad Gastein's healing waters and hot springs. You'll find me down by the wild waterfall to spark [my] immune system, shift energies, and manifest magic (it works, I promise!). Most of the spa hotels around town have the healing waters on tap, but there are many hidden locations nestled in the wilderness that locals might share with you if you ask nicely."

Today Bad Gastein is on the brink of revival, home to artists and creatives who are revitalizing its grandeur and eccentricity, embracing the draw of the thermal springs and open-air living.

# RUSSIAN & TURKISH BATHS

*A New York Institution*

EAST VILLAGE, NEW YORK, UNITED STATES

In operation since 1892, the Russian & Turkish Baths—often referred to by locals as simply "The Tenth Street Baths"—became the sole surviving bathhouse in the city after the AIDS epidemic. Today, the baths are co-owned by two families who split the business—alternating weeks of operation known as "Boris Weeks" or "David Weeks." According to local Schuyler Quin, for a while, the only way to keep track of who owned which week was to hang around long enough that they eventually gave you a business card with the full year's calendar. "Black for Boris. Red for David." It's easier to discern now and, while each owner offers an extremely different experience, one thing holds true: people from every walk of life—celebrities, artists, locals, musicians, and politicians—come to bathe because a *schvitz* (traditional Yiddish steam bath) is for everyone.

Decidedly not a luxury experience, the baths feature four steam rooms of varying intensity and a cold plunge pool and, famously, the Russian Room—an incredibly hot room that reaches 200°F [93°C], perhaps hotter depending on whose week it is. One of only a few of its kind in the United States, the Russian Room consists of 20,000 pounds [9,070 kilograms] of rock that are heated overnight, radiating an intense heat throughout the day. A central basin of frigid water flows through the center, buckets bobbing in wait. The traditional therapeutic Russian *platza* massage is administered here—a vigorous flogging with oak leaves dunked in olive-oil soap that is designed to open up the pores and remove toxins and dead skin. Following the 10- to 15-minute treatment, bathers then hobble to the well in the middle of the room to pour ice water over their heads.

The Eucalyptus Room, or aromatherapy room, is thick with steam and "the complaints of old East Village Ukrainians," according to Schuyler. "Every 12 minutes or so, an attendant dumps eucalyptus oil into the steam bucket and it's nearly impossible to breathe." Due to the high heat, no longer than 4 minutes is advised.

The Redwood Room, or "Debate Center," is a mellow 95°F [35°C], allowing bathers the ability to linger, fostering "some of the most heated philosophical discussions I have ever overheard," says Schuyler. "I've met scientists, doctors, and war criminals—they all come here to share their stories and talk about what it was like before," says Schuyler. "These baths are unlike anywhere else in the world."

If you make it through all the rooms, the last is the cold plunge, an invigorating reward before venturing back out into the city. As a 20-year bathhouse enthusiast, Jason Goodman says, "What struck me on my first visit to the baths was the way I felt on the way out the door. I felt better than I had in a long time. It took me a few visits to really understand it, but in a 185°F [85°C] sauna, the noise machine in our heads goes off and there is a truly grounding, mind-body connection that happens . . . it's hard not to be fully present in a ripping hot sauna or a very cold pool."

## Platza

"A *platza* is a whole-body treatment in a
Russian steam sauna in which a *venik*—the
Russian word for broom—made from oak,
birch, eucalyptus, or other plants is used
to push steam onto the body to open the
pores, cleanse the skin, and stimulate
circulation. Many people have never had a
*platza* before and describe the experience
as life-altering. Some people have very
intimate emotional experiences."
–Ekin Balcıoğu, co-founder of
*Hamam* magazine

# THE ROMAN BATHS

## BATH, SOMERSET, UNITED KINGDOM

Famed bathers, the ancient Romans built many thermae—bathing facilities—but the most well-preserved today are in Bath, England. Dating back to the first century CE, they were originally constructed as both a religious temple to worship the goddess Sulis Minerva—the Celtic-Roman goddess local to the area—and as a site for public bathing. Today the baths are preserved in four main features: the Sacred Spring, the Roman Temple, the Roman Bath House, and the museum. Springing from the nearby Mendip Hills, the mineral-rich waters reach temperatures of 115°F [46°C].

STRUCTURE

### Roman Thermae

Thermae, or communal baths, served many purposes in Roman life. In addition to being places where Romans could bathe and cleanse their bodies, perhaps most significantly thermae served as places for socializing, courting, and conducting business. Thermae were also important in the development of architectural innovations such as domes. The Romans elevated the bathing ritual to a near art form by modernizing the regimens they had learned from the Greeks, including oiling their skin and having the oil scraped off later with a metal tool called a strigil.

# JIMJILBANG

*"You're not really friends with someone until you've bathed naked together."*

ORIGINATING IN KOREA

Korean bathhouses, known as *mogyoktang* in their traditional form and *jimjilbang* in their modern form, are casual, indulgent, social places designed for visitors to wander through and linger in. From steam rooms, saunas, and herbal pools to ice rooms, jade rooms, and other elemental-laden rooms, Korean bathing has expanded past the harmony and austerity of Japanese *onsen* to include snack bars, entertainment rooms, and heated nap rooms.

Mentioned in texts from the fifteenth century, *mogyoktang* were originally state-supported bathhouses maintained by Buddhist monks and used for medicinal purposes. They were sex-segregated from 1429, but today they are a cultural institution enjoyed by families and the young and old alike—and they're open 24 hours a day.

*Jimjilbangs*, or K-spas as they are commonly known outside of Korea, are designed with people's well-being in mind. Guests move through the rooms, which include soaking pools of varying temperatures, showers, massage tables, scrub rooms, and plenty of places to rest.

There are two distinct areas in a *jimjilbang*—wet rooms and dry rooms. Wet rooms, which are separated by sex, feature hot and cold baths. Dry rooms are communal and include saunas, relaxation areas, *ondols*—heated floors for napping—and a snack bar. As everyone is separated by sex in the wet rooms, it's common practice to be naked here, carrying only a small hand towel and letting friends, family, or strangers help scrub you down. In the communal areas, everyone is given *jimjilbang* pajamas to wear while they lounge and sweat.

Inside the *jimjilbangs* can be found smaller traditional Korean kiln saunas, or *hanjeung-mak*. In a *hanjeungmak*, which features an intensely hot, dry heat, pine is burned in a domelike kiln made of stone. Saunas can be lined with wood, mineral rocks, crystals, stones, or metals—all elements used in traditional Korean medicine. There are also ice rooms as well as loam, stone, and clay rooms.

One of the most notable experiences of Korea's bathing culture is known as *seshin*, or scrub. This rigorous and intense exfoliation is performed by *ajummas*—older women who are naked or in (often) black lingerie who ritualistically scrub, scrape, wash, and clean bathers. The result is incredibly soft and refreshed skin.

The joy of a *jimjilbang* is that there is no specific order to follow; it is designed for people to take their time. One method you can follow is to strip, shower, bathe, take a sauna, then do a scrub and massage. As hygiene is paramount, it is crucial to shower before entering the water, and your hair should never be down.

No matter how guests decide to enjoy their time while visiting a *jimjilbang*, it's important to remember that silence is golden.

# 7132 THERME

*An Architectural Dream*
VALS, SWITZERLAND

Stone, glass, and water meet in these alpine thermal baths. Designed to re-create what it must be like to be inside a mountain, 7132 offers visitors an immersive, sensorial experience.

Built over the only thermal springs in the region, the baths are a masterwork of architectural design by Peter Zumthor. People have been visiting these healing waters since the late nineteenth century, and the venue was reimagined by Zumthor in 1996.

Made with 60,000 slabs of Vals quartzite, the monolithic structure creates an almost cathedral-like experience as one swims through the corridors, experiencing one of the eight thermal pools—including the frigid ice pool, a balmy fire pool, a flower-scented blossom pool, and a sound pool where bathers are engulfed by sound vibrations.

# CASA ETÉREA
*Mirrored Embrace*

SAN MIGUEL DE ALLENDE, GUANAJUATO, MEXICO

This isolated writer's retreat is an off-grid hideaway, sequestered among mesquite and mysteries on the mountainside of an extinct volcano. Designed "as a theater to nature," Casa Etérea encourages an interactive experience with the landscape, inviting guests to sit, soak, and steep in nature. Surrounded by dry scrub, deciduous forest, oaks, and canyons, the house is accessible only by four-wheel-drive vehicles, sitting on the slope of the Los Picachos mountains , which rise to 8,520 feet [2,600 meters] above sea level.

Inside, among jute, leather, wood, and stone, a statement copper tub sits beside the bed, looking out through floor-to-ceiling windows at the mountain behind. Built with bird-friendly mirrored glass, the exterior diffuses the liminal space between the wilds outside and the comforts within.

# SCHOONER OPAL
# OF NORTH SAILING

*A Soak and a Sail*

HÚSAVÍK, ICELAND

Sailing along Jurassic coastlines and among majestic glaciers, *Schooner Opal* is a double-masted, 79-foot [24-meter], hybrid electric tall ship. The boat, now owned and operated by North Sailing out of Húsavík, Iceland, was originally built in Damgarten, Germany, in 1951, as a fishing trawler. Captained by Heimir Harðarson, the addition of a wooden hot tub onboard Opal was Heimir's idea and installed in 2017.

Today, the ship voyages throughout the Arctic coasts of Iceland and Greenland and, according to those aboard, "You can't make a mistake by jumping in a warm hot tub at any time of day and watching the northern lights from the hot pot—while enjoying a drink—is always one of the highlights of an expedition."

Converted to a hybrid electric schooner in 2015 in an effort to lower the carbon footprint, *Opal* has ten sails, including traditional square sails. The stern of the boat features a hand-built wooden hot tub, perfect for warming up on freezing spring days or after a refreshing swim in the Arctic Ocean. The tub is warmed by an electric heater and comfortably seats eight people—but can squeeze in up to sixteen.

# HAMMAM
*Transformative Traditional Baths*
ORIGINATING IN TURKEY

For the Turks, the ritual of bathing is meant to purify the soul as much as the body. The Turkish bath, or hammam—which means "spreader of warmth" in Arabic—has existed for centuries. But it became widespread during the Ottoman Empire in the fourteenth century as they built hammams across the lands they conquered, including much of the Middle East and North Africa.

These cathedral-like structures feature large domes and ornate architecture built around a central hot stone slab where bathers prepare for the traditional five-step bathing ritual of the hammam: warming the body, massage, sloughing dead skin, soaping, and relaxation.

By moving through rooms of varying temperatures—warm, hot, and cold—the thermal circuit of a hammam is designed to allow your body to sweat, offering the opportunity to fully surrender to physical, mental, and, perhaps, spiritual relaxation.

A cultural staple modeled after the ancient Roman baths, hammams were often connected to mosques so Muslim men could bathe before their prayers. Today hammams are far more social than religious. A true hammam experience is as much about cleansing as relaxing and surrendering to your *tellak* or *natir*, the male or female attendants who guide you through the ritual. Unlike the Roman thermae, hammams are not designed for soaking or submerging. Instead, people wash by pouring buckets of water over themselves.

Ekin Balcıoğlu, cofounder of *Hamam* magazine, says that today hammams are not viewed as they once were in Turkey. "I want to change the way hammams are viewed by Turks, to restore the image they have in society." For her, when she visits, she thinks about the harmony of all the elements and temperatures coming together—the hot and cold, the air, stone, and water. "Bathing is a practice that transforms the body and changes consciousness," she says. "It's a ritual act of cleansing and when you go deeper than just basic hygiene, you realize that exposing yourself to different extreme temperatures is mind-altering."

"Communal bathing is special," Ekin says. "Being naked is a liberation . . . it's the greatest equalizer. In the *Hamam* manifesto, we say 'At the place where water and skin meet for ritualistic cleansing we declare a solemn truth: Nobody is the same, but everyone is equal and welcome.'"

This cherished bathing ritual of the hammam is performed as follows:

You begin in a warm room to slow down, arrive, and acclimate to the heat. Next, you move to a hotter room—either warmed by hot, dry air or, in a Moroccan-style hammam, one heated by warm water running through the pipes. Here, your body is scrubbed with a soap paste designed to remove impurities from the skin. Next comes the kese, a strong massage performed with sharp, rhythmic, circular motions that slough off layers of dead skin. After that, it's time to rest on a warm marble slab called a gobektaslin, where you are massaged with a thin, soapy, foam-filled cloth. Your tellak then splashes you with warm water to rinse away the soap. Last but not least, you enter the cold room to invigorate and enliven the body.

# OCEAN POOLS
## AROUND THE WORLD

Either formed as natural pools or human-made by excavating rock and reinforcing with concrete, ocean pools are filled by the tide or pumped-in seawater. Always changing, they engage in an intimate conversation with the natural world, impacted by weather, tide, and sea life. Interesting and aesthetically pleasing, ocean pools dot coastlines around the world—South Africa is known for them, as is Australia—but while some are safe for swimming, others are best left alone.

TRADITION

### *Ireland's Ancient Seaweed Baths*

Very little is known about the mysterious earth-and-stone sweathouses scattered across Ireland's rural landscape, though they are believed to have originated in Scandinavia with the Vikings. However, the Irish use of seaweed as a remedy has been well known since the twelfth century. Seaweed bathhouses dot the Atlantic coast, with people traditionally taking long, hot baths filled with ribbons of the alkaline, mineral-rich vegetation. A potent treatment for skin conditions, detoxification, and sore muscles, seaweed baths have become increasingly popular today, and seaweed is now included as an ingredient in skincare products as well as packaged at-home bathing kits.

# SHINRIN-YOKU

*Forest Bathing*

**ORIGINATING IN JAPAN**

*Shinrin-yoku*, or "forest bathing"—a term coined in 1982 by the Japanese Ministry of Agriculture, Forestry & Fisheries—is about immersing oneself in nature and finding harmony in the natural world. Part physiological and part psychological, the practice emerged in Japan as an ecological antidote to the country's tech boom and a way for people to reconnect with and protect Japan's forests.

Dr. Qing Li, author of *Forest Bathing*, says we innately know that spending time in nature is good for us. While researchers only began studying the beneficial impact of nature in the 1990s, the practice has long been recognized by many cultures—especially Indigenous ones—around the world.

Li says that the key to unlocking the power of the forest is through your five senses. First, find a spot in nature, walking aimlessly and slowly. Then let your body be your guide, allowing nature to enter you through your ears, eyes, nose, mouth, hands, and feet. "Listen to the birds, look at the [greenery], smell the fragrances, taste the air, place your hands on a tree, dip your fingers in a stream. [Experience] life on the ground. Release your sense of joy and calm; your sixth sense is your state of mind."

The intention of *shinrin-yoku* is not to exercise, like hiking or jogging. It's to simply observe and be in nature, absorbing the atmosphere of the forest through your senses.

"I love not Man the less,
 but Nature more."

—LORD BYRON

# WOOD–FIRED HOT TUBS BY GOODLAND

*The Pursuit of Pause*

VANCOUVER, BRITISH COLUMBIA, CANADA

Craig Pearce is owner and designer of Goodland, a Vancouver-based company that makes outdoor living products designed for people to enjoy the moment and forget the noise. He has spent a lot of time thinking about what makes an outdoor bathing experience so primal, and what could make it even better. "Half of the fun is the anticipation. Building the fire, watching the smoke. Planning it early in the day so you have something to look forward to later."

The process of heating a wood-fired tub—gathering the wood, stacking it, building the fire, stirring the water, and waiting for it to get hot—takes about 90 minutes using an armful of fallen limbs and brush. The ritual encourages you to slow down and connect to the nature around you.

"When we moved out to the country, we began living so closely with nature that I couldn't help but consider the impact we were having on the environment," Craig says. "How much water we were using, how much wood. I realized it wasn't about quantity anymore; it was about quality." He has purposefully incorporated this insight into every aspect of Goodland. Made from recyclable aluminum and cedar, Goodland tubs are much smaller than other wood-fired baths, which means they use less water and wood and have less of an environmental impact. "Our tubs are easy to assemble, easy to move, easy to drain, and comfortable to sit in," Craig says.

As for the perfect tub soak, he adds, "It's all about the setting. Creating meaningful moments to pause, taking a break from life's hustle and grounding oneself in nature is what it's all about. The art of enjoying free time is not a [practice] North Americans are well versed in. Work and success take priority over relaxation, bonding with each other, and connecting to nature. For us, we decided success is about pleasure over productivity."

HERE ARE PEARCE'S STEPS TO ENJOYING
YOUR OWN TUB SOAK IN NATURE:

Choose an environment that offers you
space without distraction.
Bring whatever you want to add—
salts, soap, and so on.

Be sure to keep your wood nearby so you
don't have to carry it far. We use scrap wood
and windfall whenever possible.

Take a shower before you get in so you aren't
making the water dirtier than it needs to be.

If you're somewhere that gets cold, consider
putting insulation under the tub so it holds
heat better. We suggest using rigid insulation
and just putting your tub on top of that. It will
stay hot for most of the weekend.

Consider your water source. You can use
anything from rainwater to seawater.

If you don't put chemicals in the water, use it
as gray water for plants when you're done.

Though the bathing ritual is deeply cleansing and relaxing, the act of immersing oneself in nature is rewarding in and of itself.

# COTTARS SAFARI
## MAASAI MARA, KENYA

According to Carolyn Roumeguere, who grew up living with the Maasai in Kenya, safari is a way of life and, after a long day traversing the savanna, there is nothing more welcome than a bath to wash away the sweat and dust. A remnant of colonial-era safari travel, a traditional bush bath is a canvas tent set up in the open air just outside the tent, offering the opportunity to bathe as wildlife wanders by.

# SPORANCH
*A Desert Soak in a Forest of Joshua Trees*
**JOSHUA TREE NATIONAL PARK, CALIFORNIA, UNITED STATES**

"Good things happen when you slow down long
enough to allow your heart to catch up with your body."
—FRIEND OF SPORANCH OWNER SCOTT SPORLEDER

Under the countless stars of the high desert, amid a forest of ancient Joshua trees, SpoRanch provides an escape from the speed of city life. The focus here is about slowing down, finding the pace of nature, and bathing in the untouched yucca forest, feeling the presence and energy of the land.

Minimal and sparse and completely off-grid, SpoRanch is designed to interfere with nature as little as possible. Nestled in a canyon just outside of Joshua Tree National Park, the unearthly landscape undergoes extreme temperature shifts throughout the year, making it an ever-changing and dynamic place to live in sync with.

To be sensitive to the natural environment, owner Scott Sporleder built a series of floating decks, including a bathing deck with a wood-fired hot tub. Soaking either under the night sky or in the early-morning desert light is an otherworldly, almost euphoric experience. Scott adds, "To bathe underneath these magical Joshua trees is a gift from the planet and an opportunity to allow the chatter of your mind to settle while you draw energy from the gods of the desert."

# BAINS ROMAINS DE DORRES
## LA CERDANYA, FRANCE

Nestled among the French Pyrenees mountains, the Bains Romains de Dorres—the Roman baths of Dorres—lie in a meadow above the valley, allowing visitors to soak in the ancient, granite-carved pools. The sulfur-rich water springs forth at 106°F [41°C], the hottest in the country. Used since 1500 BCE, today the baths are a welcome respite for those on the Carlit 50 Lakes Trek, hiked by locals and visitors alike.

# TAKARAGAWA ONSEN OSENKAKU
*A Monastic Refuge*

MINAKAMI, GUNMA PREFECTURE, JAPAN

Like a fairytale on the river, Takaragawa Onsen Osenkaku lies upstream of Tonegawa, on the Takara River. In the old days, this *onsen* was called Bath of the White Hawk because, according to legend, Yamato Takeru no Mikoto (the Brave Prince of Yamato) went to conquer his enemies to the east, and when he went up Mount Hotaka, he fell sick. He spotted a hawk flying in the land below and when he walked down, he saw steam rising from the ground. After soaking in the warm waters, his illness went away.

Takaragawa is located in a small town east of Nagano, immersed in nature and with thermal baths heated by the river. The baths recently became all-gendered, offering visitors the opportunity for coed bathing in addition to the women-only pools.

As with all *onsen*, be sure to follow the etiquette and guidelines of the Takaragawa *ryokan*, or traditional Japanese inn.

# CRÉ NATURAL BUILDING

*Building a Natural Desert Bath*

JOSHUA TREE NATIONAL PARK, CALIFORNIA, UNITED STATES

Bryce Ehrecke and Kelly Brown of Cré Natural Building design and create meaningful spaces and natural structures as a way to experience and connect people to place. Their work, which includes saunas, natural tubs, and shelters, interacts with the local environment in a respectful way, reflecting the inner and outer worlds as a way to care for both.

"We practice natural building, which is all there was prior to colonialism, mass transportation, and industrialization," Bryce says. "We use as much local material as possible, as close to its raw and natural form as possible, to create healthy, breathable, nontoxic, durable structures."

After apprenticing for years with a natural builder named Pat Hennebery and traveling for another year to learn from other natural builders, Bryce began to bring different traditions together in a thoughtful way, seeking alternatives to conventional building methods as a way to honor the earth rather than extract from it.

When building a sauna or tub, the same principles apply as with any structure—you must first consider the environment, the flora and fauna, and those who will interact with what is being built, both directly and indirectly. Bryce and Kelly encourage people to "consider the impact of the structure on the Indigenous peoples of the area, and find ways to either give funds or access to the land and structures in gratitude for being on their [native land], so that you can be there in a good way."

It's also important to consider additional ways of using or generating water and heat—such as through rainwater harvesting, passive cooling and heating, greenhouses, and cold frames.

"With a tub, especially an outdoor tub, a gray-water system with a mulch basin to build soil is always a good idea," Bryce says. "Definitely plan for secondary uses of the water and situate the tub in a way that connects you to nature, even if it's just having a few plants or natural elements nearby.

"As far as materials go, the aesthetic has to come down to what is available and abundant in the local environment. We have an abundance of sand where we live and not much else suitable for a tub, so we used a small amount of Portland cement so we could use what was local. Rammed earth, desert masonry, Tadelakt plasters, stone, cedar, or keeping a used tub out of landfill can all be good options.

"Soaking in the environment around you allows it to soak into you and guide all that you do," Bryce adds. "Bathing [outdoors] blurs the line between us and nature, helping us to remember there is no separation."

# SCANDINAVE SPA

*A Silent Retreat*

WHISTLER, BRITISH COLUMBIA, CANADA

With four locations across Canada, Scandinave Spa emphasizes the power of silence as a teacher and hydrotherapy as a healer. Engulfed in spruce and cedar, Scandinave Spa Whistler's Lost Lake baths are technology-free and completely silent. Through inner stillness and tuning into the senses, guests use nature as a means to self-regulation and well-being.

Scandinave's philosophy is rooted in the 1,000-year-old tradition of hydrotherapy that uses water, in all its forms, with intent as a functional, holistic treatment for pain, ailments, and relief. Their ritual uses a system of "Hot, Cold, Relax, Repeat" to soothe and energize the body and spirit, improving circulation, stimulating the lymphatic system, releasing endorphins, and integrating the direct and indirect benefits throughout.

By embracing the rustic elements of nature and blending them with state-of-the-art facilities, Scandinave fosters genuine relaxation in the heart of nature.

### FIRST, HOT
To release tension in the body and mind,
begin by increasing body temperature through
baths, sauna, and pools.

### THEN, COLD
Be brought back into the invigorating present by
immersing the body in cold—plunge, showers, air.

### RELAX
Seal it in with at least 10 to 15 minutes of doing
nothing except observing nature and thought.

### REPEAT

# AMANGIRI

*Calm in the Canyon*

CANYON POINT, BIG WATER, UTAH, UNITED STATES

At the edge of a desert valley, surrounded by mesas and mountains, landlocked and nearly lost, Amangiri is an oasis of luxurious retreat. Made of sandstone that nearly disappears into the wind swept, rugged, and wild red-rock country, Amangiri sits in the heart of Diné land, inspired and rooted in the restorative tradition of *hózhó*—a state of alignment and harmony with self and nature.

Holistic well-being puts nature at the center, embracing the four elements of wind, fire, earth, and water as the great teachers. Designed to reconnect and ground, Amangiri holds water with great respect, perhaps because of its desolate desert surroundings, creating entire pavilions around the element. In all aspects, guests are given the space to find their own sense of perspective and respite, from floating in the sensory deprivation pools—in literal darkness, with water brined so floating is effortless, and the temperature is set to match one's own body heat exactly—to visiting the steam rooms, sauna, plunge pools, and heated watsu step pool, which all curve around escarpments of sandstone rock and nature.

## PHOTOGRAPHY CREDITS

Pages 2–3: Photograph copyright © 2018 Ivan Bandura; Page 5: Photograph copyright © 2022 Jeremy Koreski, @jeremykoreski; Page 8: Photograph copyright © 2022 Ethan Abitz, @ethanabitz; Page 13: Photograph copyright © 2022 courtesy of Cedar + Stone Nordic Sauna, www.cedarandstonesauna.com; Pages 14–15: Photographs copyright © 2022 courtesy of Partisans, www.partisans.com; Page 19: Photograph copyright © 2022 Anne Nygård, www.unsplash.com/@polarmermaid; Pages 20–25: Photograph copyright © 2022 courtesy of Aleksi Hautamäki; Pages 26–29: Photograph copyright © 2022 courtesy of Panorama Glass Lodge, www.panoramaglasslodge.com; Pages 32–35: Photographs copyright © 2022 Nicolás Valdés; Pages 36–37: Photograph copyright © 2022 Stine Christiansen; Page 38: Photographs copyright © 2022 Mike Karlsson Lundgren; Page 39: Photograph copyright © 2022 Timon Wolf; Pages 40–41: Photographs copyright © 2022 Stine Christiansen; Page 42: Photograph copyright © 2022 courtesy of Cedar + Stone Nordic Sauna, www.cedarandstonesauna.com; Page 44: Photograph copyright © 2022 Scott Sporleder, @spoart; Page 45: Photograph copyright © 2022 Renee Thurston, @reneethurston_; Pages 46–49: Photographs copyright © 2022 Ilanna Barkusky, www.ilannabarkusky.com; Pages 50–55: Photographs copyright © 2022 courtesy of the Scarcity and Creativity Studio at The Oslo School of Architecture and Design; Page 56: Photograph copyright © 2022 Jaan Parmask; Page 58: Photograph copyright © 2022 Mike Pham, @phamuelphoto; Page 60: Photographs copyright © 2022 courtesy of Partisans; Pages 62–67: Photographs copyright © 2022 Jeremy Koreski, @jeremykoreski; Pages 68–71: Photographs copyright © 2022 Ali Hartwig, @alihartwig; Page 72: Photograph copyright © 2022 courtesy of Canopy & Stars , www.canopyandstars.co.uk; Page 73: Photograph copyright © 2022 Kjell Ove Storvik; Page 77: Photograph copyright © 2022 Amelia Le Brun, @amslebrun; Pages 78–79: Photographs copyright © 2022 Yaroslav Shuraev, www.pexels.com/@yaroslav-shuraev; Page 80: Photograph copyright © 2022 David Dworkind; Page 81: Photograph copyright © 2022 JoAnne Haley; Page 82: Photograph copyright © 2022 David Dworkind; Page 83: Photograph copyright © 2022 Peter Crosby, @pbcrosby; Pages 84–85: Photographs copyright © 2022 Dag Jenssen, courtesy of Visit Dalen and Tokke Kommune; Pages 86–87: Photographs copyright © 2022 Isbading Synne Aasland, courtesy of Visit Dalen and Tokke Kommune; Pages 88–91: Photographs copyright © 2022 courtesy of Arctic Bath & Spa, www.arcticbath.se; Pages 92–93: Photographs copyright © 2022 Spencer Davis; Page 97: Photograph copyright © 2022 Dana Halferty, www.danahalferty.com; Pages 98–100: Photographs copyright © 2022 Laura Austin, @laura_austin; Page 101: Top photograph copyright © 2022 Laura Austin, @laura_austin, bottom photograph copyright @ 2022 Lindsey Bro; Page 103: Photograph copyright © 2022 Laura Austin, @laura_austin; Pages 104–107: Photograph copyright © 2022 Megan Anderson; Page 108: Photograph copyright © 2022 courtesy Ainsworth Hot Springs, www.ainsworthhotsprings.com; Page 109: Photograph copyright © 2022 Ami Illingsworth; Page 110: Photograph copyright © 2022 Colin Watts; Page 112: Top photograph copyright © 2022 iStock.com/ColobusYeti, bottom photograph copyright © 2022 iStock.com/Focus_on_Nature; Page 113: Top photograph copyright © 2022 iStock.com/rusm, bottom photograph copyright © 2022 iStock.com/wiesdie; Page 114: Photograph copyright © 2022 Anna Shvets; Page 116: Left photograph copyright © 2022 Anna Shvets, middle photograph copyright © 2022 Uğurcan Özmen; Page 117: Photograph copyright © 2022 Anna Shvets; Pages 118–23: Photograph copyright © 2022 Scott Sporleder, @spoart; Page 124: Photograph copyright © 2022 courtesy of Termas Geométricas, termasgeometricas.cl; Page 126: Photograph copyright © 2022 Klaudia Poloncová, @klaudipoloncova; Page 128: Top left, top right, bottom right photographs copyright © 2022 Klaudia Poloncová, bottom left photograph copyright © 2022 Daniel Cox; Page 129: Photograph copyright © 2022 Klaudia Poloncová; Pages 130–33: Photographs copyright © 2022 courtesy of Sky Lagoon by Pursuit, www.skylagoon.com; Page 134: Photograph copyright © 2022 iStock.com/Yu Sun; Page 135: Photograph copyright © 2022 Marianna Jamadi, @nomadic_habit; Pages 136–39: Photographs copyright © 2022 Mike

Pham, @phamuelphoto; Pages 140–43: Photographs copyright © 2022 Spencer Davis; Pages 144–47: Photographs copyright © 2022 Julian DeSchutter, @deshoots; Pages 148–50: Photographs copyright © 2022 Marianna Jamadi, @nomadic_habit; Pages 151–53: Photograph copyright © 2022 Dana Halferty, www.danahalferty.com; Page 154: Photograph copyright © 2022 Tanzy Owen; Page 155: Photograph copyright © 2022 Melissa Chaquea; Pages 156–57: Photographs copyright © 2022 Martaan van den Heuvel; Pages 158–59: Photographs copyright © 2022 Laura Austin, @laura_austin; Page 160: Photograph copyright © 2022 courtesy of Termas Cacheuta, www.termascacheuta.com; Page 161: Photograph copyright © 2022 courtesy of Peninsula Hot Springs, www.peninsulahotsprings.com; Page 162: Photograph copyright © 2022 Callen Hearne; Pages 164–65: Photograph copyright © 2022 Camrin Dengel, www.camrindengel.com; Page 166: Photograph copyright © 2022 Natalie Gildersleeve; Pages 168–69: Photographs copyright © 2022 Scott Sporleder, @spoart; Page 173: Photograph copyright © 2022 Amelia Le Brun, @amslebrun; Pages 174–75: Photographs copyright © 2022 iStock.com/Casanowe; Page 175: Photographs copyright © 2022 iStock.com/Casanowe; Page 176: Top photograph copyright © 2022 iStock.com/golfcphoto, bottom right photograph copyright © 2022 Thom Fougere, bottom left photograph copyright © 2022 Lucas Calloch; Page 178: Photograph copyright © 2022 @bungee-ride, Creative Commons, www.flickr.com/photos/slackrhackr/; Page 179: Photograph copyright © 2022 iStock.com/Lcc54613; Page 180: Photograph copyright © 2022 Scott David Hansche; Page 181: Photograph copyright © 2022 Joann Pai, @sliceofpai, www.sliceofpai.com; Page 182: Photograph copyright © 2022 iStock.com/LaChouettePhoto; Page 183: Photograph copyright © 2022 Adriano Batista, @adriano.fy; Pages 184–87: Photographs copyright © 2022 courtesy of A Bath House, www.abathhouse.com; Pages 188–91: Photographs copyright © 2022 courtesy of Sanduny, www.sanduny.ru; Page 192: Clockwise from top left: photograph copyright © 2022 Nadin Brendel, @thequietquest; photograph copyright © 2022 REGINA Hotel, @reginahotel; photograph copyright © 2022 Nadin Brendel, @visitbadgastein; photograph copyright © 2022 Nadin Brendel, @thecoverse.co; Page 194: Photograph copyright © 2022 courtesy of Villa Excelsior, @villaexcelsior; Page 195: Photograph copyright © 2022 courtesy of Felsentherme Bad Gastein, @felsenthermebadgastein; Pages 196–201: Photographs copyright © 2022 Nicole Craine, www.nicolecraine.com; Page 202: Photograph copyright © 2022 Rachel Claire; Pages 204–7: Photographs copyright © 2022 Lindsey Bro; Pages 208–11: Photographs copyright © 2022 courtesy of Global Image Creation – 7132 Hotel, Vals; Page 213: Photograph copyright © 2022 Prashant Ashoka; Page 214: Photograph copyright © 2022 Ása Steinars; Page 216: Photographs copyright © 2022 Aleš Mucha; Page 217: Photograph copyright © 2022 Arngrímur Arnarson; Page 218: Photograph copyright © 2022 iStock.com/FSYLN; Page 220: Photograph copyright © 2022 Dorsa Masghati; Page 221: Top photograph copyright © 2022 Laura Ausin, bottom photograph copyright © 2022 iStock.com/diegograndi; Page 222: Photograph copyright © 2022 iStock.com/javi_indy; Page 223: Photograph copyright © 2022 iStock.com/master2; Pages 224–25: Photograph copyright © 2022 Mike Pham, @phamuelphoto; Pages 226–29: Photographs copyright © 2022 Dallas Hartwig, @dallashartwig; Pages 230–33: Photographs copyright © 2022 courtesy of Goodland, hellogoodland.com; Pages 234–35: Photographs copyright © 2022 Dave Krugman, @davekrugman; Pages 236–38: Photographs copyright © 2022 Scott Sporleder, @spoart; Page 239: Photograph copyright © 2022 Gerard Moral; Pages 240–43: Photographs copyright © 2022 courtesy of Takaragawa Onsen Osenkaku; Pages 244–47: Photographs copyright © 2022 Kelly Brown, @kellybrownphoto; Page 248: Photograph copyright © 2022 courtesy of Scandinave Spa Whistler; Pages 250–53: Photographs copyright © 2022 courtesy Aman Resorts; Page 256: Photograph copyright © 2022 Laura Austin, @laura_austin.

# REFERENCES

Arnold, Spencer. "Letting Go with Hamam Magazine." Bathing Culture. December 10, 2020. https://bathingculture.com/blogs/our-story/letting-go-with-hamam-magazine.

Bath House. https://www.abathhouse.com/. Accessed April 16, 2022.

Blue Lagoon Iceland. "About Us." Accessed April 11, 2022. https://www.bluelagoon.com/about.

DiNicolantonio, James. The Longevity Solution: Rediscovering Centuries-Old Secrets to a Healthy, Long Life. Canada: Victory Belt Publishing, 2019.

Discover Dominica. "Nature's Ultimate Relaxation: Dominica's Incredible Hot Springs." May 4, 2022. https://discoverdominica.com/en/posts/17/natures-ultimate-relaxation-dominicas-incredible-hot-springs.

Dworkin, David. Quoted in Marissa Hermanson, "A Timber-Clad Prefab Cabin Offers Respite in the Canadian Wilderness." Last modified October 9, 2020. https://www.dwell.com/article/hinterhouse-menard-dworkind-architecture-design-00db3d5a.

Esalen. www.esalen.org. Accessed April 16, 2022.

Fitzgerald, Sunny. "The Secret to Mindful Travel? A Walk in the Woods." National Geographic, October 18, 2019. https://www.nationalgeographic.com/travel/article/forest-bathing-nature-walk-health.

Hamam. https://hamammag.com/.

Hautamäki, Aleksi. "Project Ö: The Ultimate Self-Sufficient Escape: In Conversation with Aleksi Hautamäki." By Kobu. Published May 7, 2021. https://kobu.co/project-o/.

"Hot Springs/Geothermal Features." US National Parks. Accessed April 22, 2022. https://www.nps.gov/subjects/geology/hot-springs.htm.

Laukkanen, Jari A., Tanjaniina Laukkanen, and Setor K. Kunutsor. "Cardiovascular and Other Health Benefits of Sauna Bathing: A Review of the Evidence." Mayo Clinic Proceedings 93, no. 8 (August 2018):1111–1121. https://doi.org/10.1016/j.mayocp.2018.04.008.

Li, Qing. "The Key To Unlocking the Power of the Forest Is in the Five Senses." Time, May 18, 2018. https://time.com/5259602/japanese-forest-bathing/.

Li, Qing. Forest Bathing: How Trees Can Help You Find Health and Happiness. New York: Penguin, April 2018.

"Mineral Hot Springs Types." Hot Springs Locator. Accessed April 22, 2022. https://hotspringslocator.com/mineral-hot-spring-types.

Molvar, Kari, ed. Be Well: New Spa and Bath Culture and the Art of Being Well. Berlin: Gestalten, May 2020.

Mountain Culture Group. "Whitecap Alpine Has Revealed Its New Sauna and Its [sic] Awesome." Accessed April 8, 2022. https://mountainculturegroup.com/whitecap-alpine-lakeside-sauna-revealed/.

Nichols, Wallace J. "'Blue Mind': Why Being near the Water Makes You Happy." By Marla Cimini. USA Today, November 13, 2017. https://www.usatoday.com/story/travel/destinations/2017/11/13/blue-mind/857903001/.

Nichols, Wallace J. Blue Mind: The Surprising Science That Shows How Being near, in, on, or under Water Can Make You Happier, Healthier, More Connected, and Better at What You Do. New York: Back Bay Books, 2015.

Nimmo Bay. https://nimmobay.com/. Accessed April 16, 2022.

Parachini, Allan. "Aquatic Attraction: Poets, Pragmatists and Scholars Ponder the Inexplicable Appeal of Being Near Water." Los Angeles Times, April 7, 1989. https://www.latimes.com/archives/la-xpm-1989-04-07-vw-1198-story.html.

Patrick, Rhonda. "Sauna." Accessed April 10, 2022. https://www.foundmyfitness.com/topics/sauna.

Patrick, Rhonda. "Cold Exposure Therapy." Accessed April 10, 2022. https://www.foundmyfitness.com/topics/cold-exposure-therapy.

Ramos, Amanda. "Talks with the Women of Driftwood Sauna." Bathing Culture. March 24, 2021. https://bathingculture.com/blogs/our-story/talks-with-the-women-of-driftwood-sauna.

Rusk, Tom. Quoted in Allan Parachini, "Aquatic Attraction: Poets, Pragmatists and Scholars Ponder the Inexplicable Appeal of Being Near Water." Los Angeles Times, April 7, 1989. https://www.latimes.com/archives/la-xpm-1989-04-07-vw-1198-story.html.

Sheldon Chalet. "Historic Sheldon Mountain House." Accessed April 8, 2022. https://sheldonchalet.com/history/.

Sood, Suemedha. "The Origins of Bathhouse Culture Around the World." BBC, November 29, 2012. https://www.bbc.com/travel/article/20121129-the-origins-of-bathhouse-culture-around-the-world.

Suleskarvegen. https://suleskarvegen.no/en/what-to-see/soria-moria-sauna/. Accessed April 16, 2022.

"Sweat Lodge." The Pluralism Project, Harvard University. https://pluralism.org/sweat-lodge.

"The Standard Guide to Global Bathing Cultures." The Standard, February 20, 2018. https://www.standardhotels.com/culture/bathing-cultures-hydrotherapy-rituals-Finnish-Japanese-Russian-Korean-Turkish.

Vuorenjuuri, Martti. Sauna kautta aikojen [Sauna through the ages]. Helsinki: Otava, 1967.

"What Is a Sauna Whisk?" World of Sauna, August 6, 2021. https://worldofsauna.com/what-is-a-sauna-whisk/.

## ACKNOWLEDGMENTS

To Leigh Saffold, Rachel Hiles, Vanessa Dina, Frank Brayton, and Chronicle Books, without your vision, dedication, and guidance, this book wouldn't exist—thank you for helping me put something beautiful into the world. To all the incredible photographers, thank you for your generosity, kindness, and talent. What a gift it is to witness the way you see the world. To all who shared their special places, stories, and traditions, thank you. I am still humbled by it all—the conversations and the shared experiences—and with being trusted to give shape to something we all hold so dear. To the ancestors, our wild lands, and to those who came before, thank you for stewarding these healing practices so we can continue to carry them on. To my friends and family, thank you so much for listening to everything I learned; to going on many a mission faraway, and for visiting all the countless saunas, springs, and bathhouses along the way. You made it all more fun than I'm sure it had any right to be. And to you, thank you for reading and, hopefully, keeping these stories and traditions alive. I hope you stay so very warm.

## ABOUT THE AUTHOR

As a writer, creative, and traveler, Lindsey Bro has spent much of her life finding places faraway and undiscovered. Seeking the playful as well as the profound, she sits sauna and bathes in beautiful spaces whenever possible. Lindsey started and runs @cabinlove on Instagram and can be found at www.lindseybro.com. She is currently based in Southern California.

LeMonds Aveda Salon - Spa
195 N Old Litchfield Rd
Litchfield Park, AZ 85340